RELIGIONS OF UNBELIEF

Author of *La Piété Grecque*

Le Dilemme Aristotélicien

Philosophy in the Making

Rationalisme et Religion

Co-author of *Le Charme d'Athènes*

SCIENCE AND CULTURE SERIES
JOSEPH HUSSLEIN, S.J., Ph.D., GENERAL EDITOR

RELIGIONS
of
UNBELIEF

ANDRÉ BREMOND, S.J.

*Professor of Philosophy,
Maison Saint-Louis,
Jersey, England*

THE BRUCE PUBLISHING COMPANY
MILWAUKEE

Nihil obstat: J. M. LeBlond, Jersey
Imprimi potest: Marcellus Bith, Vice Provincial, Paris
Nihil obstat: H. B. Ries, Censor librorum
Imprimatur: ✠ Samuel A. Stritch, Archiepiscopus Milwaukiensis
February 14, 1939

PREFACE BY THE GENERAL EDITOR

INTERNATIONALLY KNOWN FOR HIS CONTRIBU-
tions to French and English philosophic and cultural literature, André Bremond discusses here the present-day rationalistic prejudice which prevents many from acknowledging a
God or any divine principle transcending human reason.
Religion, to be acceptable in these circles, must somehow
eschew every form of revelation and mystery; it must keep
strictly within the limits of man's own fallible and unaided
intelligence; and it must well beware to make no demands on
human conduct or morality that are based on any other norm
than common experience. Faith in the prophets of rationalism, whose affirmations often baffle understanding, may be
commendable, but faith in God is treason.

These are at least some of the first postulates of rationalism.

Credence, we need hardly add, may never be given by its
followers to any "arbitrary" divine intervention in the course
of history. A cosmic god, however, outside the range of human
interests and unconcerned with man, may be admitted and
conveniently ignored. That, at least, would be the generous
concession some are readily prepared to make.

Rejecting with all possible emphasis the God of Sinai and
the Divine Christ of the Gospels, rationalism has made unto
itself its own gods. Man, obviously, cannot be without some
religion, or else he will seek a substitute in superstition or
make-believe. Bolshevism, grossly materialistic in its rationalism, lost no time in exhibiting for veneration and endless
national pilgrimages the cunningly embalmed body of Lenin,
magnificently enshrined in his monumental stone tomb. The

more idealistic forms of rationalism were no less prompt in directly creating their own divinities. Thus, there is the god of Spinoza, god of geometrical necessity; the god of Brunschvicg, god of scientists and philosophers we are told; the god of H. G. Wells, a romantic Manichean deity; and finally, to proceed no further, the rather sadly bedraggled and befuddled god of Bertram Russell, god of "the freeman's worship." All these the author deals with or touches upon.

Obviously there has been here a mental rebound back to the era of the old pagan who comfortably squatted by his fireside and carved out an idol after his own heart's design, to color it with ochre, and set it in the corner of his dingy cell where the leaping flame might flash its light upon it and the shadows swallow it up.

His method, if not less futile, strikes us as at least more honest than that of his modern imitators. Besides, in his own bewildered way, he doubtless did believe in a divinity immeasurably beyond the poor carven idol in its niche. His religion was still a good step ahead of rationalism. Far as he was from the wellspring of infallible truth, he drank at his own muddied pool but gave recognition to a power beyond that of man. His creed was unsophisticated.

It is the pride of modern rationalists to profess kinship of spirit to the old Greek masters, the poets, dramatists, and philosophers of Hellas, as having anticipated their own attitude of mind. In this they are greatly wrong. Nothing could have been further removed from Greek thought and life than the unhappy self-sufficiency of the modern rationalistic creed. That important point the author makes abundantly clear, and it is well that he opens his volume with this very subject. If any man there was who understood "the legacy of Greece" that man was Paul. His own approach to the men of Athens, in the midst of their Areopagus, was precisely by way of their Unknown God, and by citation from their poets.

Again, it is the method of rationalism to claim all science for its own exclusive purview. The second assertion is as groundless as the first. Not less light but more, is the incessant demand the Church makes of science.

No, Catholicism did not break the Hellenic spell. The Church preserved, applied, and sublimised it into something still more fair. For the Pantheon of the gods it gave the Cathedral of Rheims. In the same way the Church is in fullest harmony with all true aims of science, and eager to accept every least and last ion of scientific discovery, surcharged with new and vital facts. More light, more life, more beauty — spiritually and intellectually — the Church desires for mankind and is anxious to give them. Uncircumscribed Light, Unending Life, Infinite Intelligence: that is the shrine she worships at, here and hereafter.

Poor rationalism! Poor materialism! With their Spinozan god and their lifeless corpse of Lenin whose life ended in idiocy. The irony of the Almighty!

We may just mention here, without enlarging on it, a modern idealistic attempt at a Religion without a personal God proposed by its author, the French philosopher Brunschvicg, as the one "Religion of the Spirit." What he means by "Spirit" is Scientific Reason. Enough to say that it results in human reason enshrining itself as an object of worship.

Further development of this philosophy of extreme idealistic rationalism, with its rapier play of dialectics and lack of sound, substantial principles, would be equally senseless and bewildering in a work like the present intended for English-speaking countries. Those interested will find an adequate treatment of it, on the religious side, in the author's *Rationalisme et Religion* which first suggested the RELIGIONS OF UNBELIEF wherein some parts of the former volume have been rendered or adapted by him. Father Bremond, it may incidentally be mentioned here, has written numerous books and articles touching upon religion as connected both with literature and philosophy.

Present-day reactions against religion, he rightly contends, resolve themselves ultimately into reactions against false presentations of religion that have been made to the people or to the world of learning. In the words of Canon Guy Rogers quoted by the author: "the bitter hatred is that of the betrayed and outraged lover." Our age is no longer such as Matthew Arnold depicted his own to have been. "The time for poetic melancholy has passed. There is nothing wistful about the ordinary man. In his view the situation needs radical treatment. God for him is the alternative to chaos. God is the eternal affirmation in a world of doubt."

Today and always the need of humanity is for a personal God, transcendent and immanent, without and within us, a supreme divine ruler, judge of life and death, to whom normal man can turn, whose Fatherhood he acknowledges, whose kindly Providence he implores, from whom with penitent heart, in the spirit of faith and hope and love, he confidently expects fulfillment of all His promises and the boon of a blessed eternity with Him. "Give us God!" is indeed the clamour rising from the deepest depths of the hearts of men.

Joseph Husslein, S.J., Ph.D.,
General Editor, Science and Culture Series

St. Louis University,
February 26, 1939

INTRODUCTION

OUR PURPOSE IN THIS BOOK IS TO EXAMINE AND discuss the attitude of modern rationalism towards religion, and especially towards certain attempts to supersede traditional and revealed religion by giving full satisfaction to the highest mystic and moral needs of the human soul without it.

By rationalism we mean any system which claims to be a complete interpretation and philosophy of life, both theoretical and moral, through reason alone, excluding *a priori* anything, be it event or person or dogma, which is not either a fact of common experience or a purely rational conclusion.

Such a philosophy is not necessarily deliberately atheistic. But it will not tolerate any supreme being whose attributes and dealings with the universe cannot be known and demonstrated by necessity of reason. It is, consequently, opposed to the idea of a personal God freely intervening and manifesting Himself at a given time and place, in the history of the world which He has freely created. God, if there is a God, must be rational and entirely bound by the laws of reason. Logically, then, there would be no religion but rationalism itself, and rationalism has the right to assume the name of religion if it preserves the moral values, the uplifting and moralising power which are commonly associated with popular, positive, historical, and not exclusively rational religion.

That rationalism is such, and is religion itself, while all other systems of traditional beliefs, dogmatic Christianity in particular, are superstition, idolatry, and even rank atheism, was the theory put forth a few years ago in a meeting of the Société Francaise de Philosophie by L. Brunschvicg, a prom-

inent professor at the Sorbonne in Paris. The debate begun
in the Société de Philosophie was continued in different
philosophical periodicals under the title "Querelle de l'Athé-
isme." Well-known Catholic thinkers, Gilson, Gabriel Marcel,
and others took an active part in it. The issue was hardly
favourable to the original thesis. It had the merit of bringing
to the fore the human fact of religion and the religious need
of the times; a fact which a philosophy worthy of the name
could not leave aside any longer, and a need which ought to
be supplied, if not rationally, then in some suprarational,
supernatural way.

The central point of the discussion is neatly put by Brunschvicg, quoting a well-known passage of Pascal, but reversing
the meaning. Pascal says in his *Mémorial:*

> God of Abraham, God of Isaac, God of Jacob, not of the
> philosophers and of the scientists.[1]

M. Brunschvicg, taking up these words and making them
the target of his opposition, says:

> God (the true, the only God) is the God of the philos-
> opher and the man of science, not the God of Abraham or
> the God of any "revelation" in any country, to anybody.

We must bear in mind that for Brunschvicg philosophy is
only the ultimate interpretation of science and is bound up
with science. So the one God is the one towards whom the
progress of science from Descartes to Einstein is ever pointing,
the God of the Spirit; and His religion is the Religion of the
Spirit.

In illustration of this we shall offer a study and discussion of
Spinoza's "theology," for Spinoza is acknowledged by L. Brunschvicg himself as the originator of a rationalistic religion.

Before speaking of Spinoza, it will be worth our while to
examine an objection to revealed religion and especially to
Christian dogma, drawn from the alleged fact of a thoroughly

---

[1] *Dieu d'Abraham, Dieu d'Isaac, Dieu de Jacob, non des philosophes et
des savants.*

rationalistic Hellenism. Since Hellenism was the essence of Greek thought, and since Greek civilisation was a philosophy of life and gave birth to the highest manifestations of human genius in art, literature, and philosophy, its antisupernatural spirit would carry great weight in the matter, if it were a well-authenticated fact. But is it a fact? I think we shall be able to show, against a too common prejudice, that the historical and religious evidence points rather to a deep sense of the limits and shortcomings of human reason and man's dependence on some supernatural power and goodness; that Hellenism, in a word, far from opposing the possibility of a divine message, actually expects and prepares the way for it.

To the study of European rationalism we have added here a chapter on rationalism and religion in British Philosophy or Literature, selecting two examples of religious rationalism less on account of their philosophical value than of their likely influence on the public at large. Those discussions, necessarily incomplete, form only the negative part of the work.

In the last chapters we shall try to show the rational antecedent probability of a divine manifestation of God to man to teach him the secret of his divine destiny; or in other words, how a certain fulness and intensity of moral life anticipates a divine message of salvation and disposes our soul to welcome it with joy. We have derived great help and profit for that positive part from two important books, one from England, the other from America: *The Faith of a Moralist* by A. W. Taylor, and *The Meaning of God in Human Experience* by W. E. Hocking.

Before entering upon our subject attention may be called to a study of the word *religion* and its different meanings given in the Appendix. It enables us to state as clearly as possible what the rationalist means when he speaks of a purely rational religion, or even of religion without God.

ACKNOWLEDGEMENTS

The author wishes to express his gratitude to the friends who helped him in the difficult task of translation and adaptation, especially to the Reverend C. Dolan, S.J. Ulterior changes and some suppressions have been made to suit the dispositions of a wider reading public, for which I am thankful to the Editor of the Science and Culture Series.

CONTENTS

PAGE

Preface by the General Editor vii

Introduction xi

CHAPTER

1. Was Greek Thought Rationalistic? 1

2. The Religion of Spinoza 45

3. Bertrand Russell's Religion Without God . . . 69

4. Wells' Invisible King 84

5. Religion and the Scientific Age 97

6. God and History 108

7. Religion, Personal Salvation, and History . . . 131

8. Conclusion: "Give Us God!" 143

Appendix

Meaning of the Word "Religion" 153

Index 161

xv

CHAPTER ONE

WAS GREEK THOUGHT RATIONALISTIC?

THOSE WHO ADVOCATE RATIONALISM AS GIVING
full satisfaction to the ethical and religious needs of human
nature think they find their strongest argument in the history
of classical Greece. Their contention can be summed up in a
few words:

"Greek culture was the most complete and perfect that
ever was, ensuring the fullest and happiest development of
man's powers of body and mind. It had its religious side;
gods, temples, liturgy. Nay, religion was the visible center
and the secret soul of Greek life. But that religion, under the
pleasant veil of mythology, was nothing but the divinisation
and the worship of what is most excellent in human nature:
reason. It did not acknowledge any divinity besides or beyond
the ken and laws of reason. It excluded belief in a divine
spontaneity, rationally unaccountable, exerting absolute and
imprevisible rule over the individual man's destiny. In short,
as compared with the Christian faith in God, Creator and
Redeemer, Greek religion was a *religion of unbelief*. It was
in the common people unconscious rationalism and it found
its perfect expression in the rationalism of the Philosophers."

Such, in substance, is the contention of many modern
writers, and especially of a French historian of Philosophy,
Emile Bréhier, whom we shall here consider as speaking for
this class. I think it worth our while, therefore, to consider

the case closely, falling back upon reason and investigation
to find how exactly these statements square with the facts
observed, and making the necessary distinctions, which a too
confident and somewhat fanatical, and superstitious rationalism is apt to overlook.

The modern attitude here described recalls to mind an
edict of the Emperor Julian, forbidding the use of the
classics in Christian schools. The spirit is precisely the same;
only our modern Julian has no imperial authority to
enforce his prohibition. In theory he is even more radically
rationalistic than Julian, who at least had a sense of divine
mystery. Such a prohibition, said the emperor, amounted to
a service rendered to both Christians and pagans. It prevented
the spirit of the one from being corrupted by the other. A
Christian commenting on the pagan poets, he argued, would
necessarily alter the authentic interpretation of his own
sacred books, the Old Testament and the Gospel; while
on the other hand, trying to Christianise the poets in spite
of themselves, he would spoil their meaning and break the
spell of the poetry. Let Christian and pagan each hold to
his own books.

But in spite of Julian the mutual interaction of Greek
and Christian thought could not be stopped. And in spite of
modern rationalists the fact remains undeniable that the
greatest and holiest Christian Doctors have successfully managed to baptise that literature and philosophy in which they
themselves had at least partially been brought up. The Greek
Fathers were in their times almost the only representatives of
Greek culture, and St. Augustine is, so to speak, a Platonician
to the core.

To Victorinus, a prominent scholar of Neoplatonism and
translator of Plotinus, the Gospel and the teaching of the
Church were a divine fulfilment of the highest human
wisdom, that of Plato. Before his conversion, he had been
wont to declare to his priest friend Simplicianus: "I am a
Christian, you know." But Simplicianus answered: "I will not

look upon you as a Christian until I shall have met you in the Church of Christ." To this Victorinus retorted: "Is it then the walls that make the Christian?" Yet in the end he went to that Church, entered into those walls and there made a public profession of the Faith. Nor did that mean for him a renunciation of all he had learned and taught about the Greek masters. For him as for Simplicianus and St. Augustine (who surely had some knowledge of the genuine Christian spirit) Platonism could serve as an introduction to the Gospel. Not a necessary introduction, of course. Confucius might do the same for a Chinese.

M. Bréhier's contention is not new. In Croiset's *History of Greek Literature,* which is considered as a classical work in France, I find the same rationalistic view neatly and decisively expressed:

> Hellenic culture is rationalistic and aristocratic. It consists in the apotheosis of moderate human appetite, in a rational rule of natural ambitions and desires.
>
> The Christian message was destined to find a hearty welcome in all those who were in fact excluded from the benefit of that culture, that is to say, the multitude. . . . It answered the deepest needs of the innumerable people who were left outside of that culture.

In fact, were we to believe this author, one culture was to be the death of the other:

> Christianity withered Hellenism to the root; and indeed it could not but do so. In consequence, the attempt to save Hellenism from ruin through incorporation in the new doctrine, was doomed to failure.

The alliance prepared by Clement of Alexandria and Origen could, according to this school of thought, not last. It was contrary to the very nature of things:

> The genuine Hellenic education implied belief in reason's power, in the value of sensible bodily beauty, in the goodness of the highest human ambitions, in the value of our best earthly interests, independently of any superior consideration. Emptied of that belief, it was utterly barren.

In a word, Hellenism is interpreted as meaning the sense and appreciation of merely human perfection, and further, the enjoyment of that perfection to the full. Hellenism, briefly, could be described quite completely in the words of the Greek poet:

> Ever happy Erechteides, with the constant
>   blessing of fortune;
> Children of the gods, born of this very earth
> Holy and inviolate, your food pure wisdom,
> Lightly stepping through the bright and
>   luminous aether. . . .

And what the chorus here suggest about the Athenian Erechteides is held to be true in general of the elect of Greek genius. They breathe the divine ether. Wisdom is theirs, and joy. Above all the gods, their own reason is divine. Their human virtues are idealised; they have no other gods. And they are not bound by any transcendent divine law. They have no sense of divine commandment or of absolute duty. Their rule of good and evil is an innate good taste, a sort of infallible appreciation of the right measure in the use of the passions.

Thus pictured they are thorough humanists, lovers, and worshippers of human nature, of its virtues and also of its fine passions. As the gothic broken arch is a symbol of divine transcendence, so the Greek temple, with its low pediment, is represented as being the most pleasant and noble of human dwellings and nothing more.

This prejudice about Greek culture is very widespread. By no one is it made out to be more antagonistic to the Christian spirit than by M. Bréhier. Here, for instance, is what he says in an introduction to Plotinus' treatise against the Gnostics:

> What Plotinus mostly objects to in the Gnostics is the fundamentally anti-Hellenistic, and, one might say, Christian character of their doctrine.

And to dispel all doubt as to this supposed opposition of

Hellenism, not merely to an interpretation of the Gospels, but
to the very spirit of Christianity, he adds:

> That treatise, then, has a deep meaning, far beyond the
> historic circumstances which gave it birth. It is one of the
> finest and boldest protestations of Greek Rationalism
> against that kind of religious individualism [the exclusive
> attention to men's private needs as they are supposed to be
> dependent on the arbitrary providence of some divinity]
> which was then spreading through the Greco-Roman world.
> The debate was about the right which man assumes of
> spoiling the rational view of the world by introducing into
> it fanciful and irrational powers to answer the selfish desire
> of personal salvation. There was in that attitude of mind a
> lack of moral and intellectual dignity which Plotinus could
> not but resent, as in modern times Spinoza's mind was hurt
> by such Christian dogmas as broke the continuity of the
> universe. Plotinus does not fight against some particular
> fancies of a sect; he goes straight to the principle [the essen-
> tially Christian principle], that is, the exaltation of indi-
> vidual belief and salvation [above and beyond the scientific,
> regular, rational order of the Universe]. To that he strongly
> opposes the old Hellenic tradition, according to which the
> end of man is to know and hold his true place in the uni-
> versal system of things, instead of assuming in it a privileged
> place and function.

This is perfectly clear. In exact opposition to the *haute
tenue intellectuelle et morale* of Hellenic thought, that is, in
opposition to the very dignity and nobility of human thought,
and to the philosophy in which it finds its expression, is not
only such or such an obscure sect, long since forgotten, but
the entire Christian spirit of St. Augustine and St. Paul and of
Christ Himself. So, indeed, we must interpret these words if
the history of Jesus crucified and risen from the dead is indeed
accepted as the very substance of living Christianity, and not
as a mere historical setting which could have been altogether
different.

It would seem then, that Philosophy itself, regarded as the
religion of the mind, is thus opposed diametrically to historical, revealed religion. And yet there *are* believers who
think themselves philosophers.

The great debate, started some years ago, is still being carried on: Just what meaning are we to attach to the phrase "Christian Philosophy"? Is there such a thing as an essentially Christian philosophy? Even Catholic thinkers do not perfectly agree on that point. They all must hold that no true philosophy can ever conflict with Christian belief, no more than any other science. But as philosophy is by definition an entirely rational discipline, why should it be more Christian than any other science?

On the other hand, however, it has as its object "the Whole"; or better, man and his destiny in its relation to the Whole; man and God. Philosophy, if begun with the sole help of the reason, cannot but tend to the fulness of truth about God and man. And as that truth is contained in the mysteries proposed to our faith, philosophy is extended to dogma, and finds, that though it can never reach revealed truth as a rational conclusion, still, if pursued in perfect good faith, it is sure to leave human reason on the threshold of mystery, unsatisfied and expecting or hoping for some divine manifestation. Finally, in the present state of fallen human nature, we find that the Christian mystery alone, when proposed to our faith, is able to give full satisfaction to our innate moral needs. And so some contend that not only is there a Christian philosophy, but that there is no other philosophy.

It is not my intention to enter into the controversy. But it is interesting to note the attitude of M. Bréhier in the debate. He took the occasion to repeat and insist upon his previous declarations that there is a necessary antagonism between Christian belief and Greek philosophical thought.

In his article entitled "Philosophie Chretienne," in *Revue de Métaphysique et de Morale* (1931), he says:

> For the Greek, the real object of philosophy is to discover the order of things, or the *cosmos:* each being, then, [and especially the dominating forces of nature, God and the soul] should be defined by the exact and *ne varietur* place which it occupies in this eternal order.

The order of the world, he tells us, is necessarily eternal and unchanging. The idea of a world created in time by divine free will, he continues, is to the Greeks an absurdity and a scandal. And inversely, what Greek reason considers as a rational necessity; namely, the world's eternity, is, from the Christian point of view, rank heresy.

> The assertion that the world is eternal and that its order is unchangeable, gives full satisfaction to [the Greek's] reason and love of beauty; but it is shocking to the Christian mind, and is the worst of Hellenic heresies. It amounts to a refusal to admit in the course of mundane things a real divine history, with imprevisible interventions of divine and human liberty, such as Creation, man's sin, and Redemption.

Again, on page 147, he speaks of the

> antinomy between Hellenic reason and its regular process by clear-cut ideas, and the Christian divine romance of persons acting in a supernatural [and therefore non-rational] and unforeseeable manner.

We are grateful to the learned historian for an antinomy so clearly put. It will be easier to discuss it. And discuss it we must. Are we to consider ourselves bound, as Christians, to abandon altogether the "legacy of Greece"? Must we burn what we have so eagerly admired; all that poetry and wisdom which is thoroughly pagan, *totum in maligno.* Must the believer, if he wants to remain a Christian, break the Hellenic spell?

We need not fear. Such abjuration is not at all consonant with the most authentic Christian tradition. Let us use our *reason* and consider the matter closely. And first, I beg to retain from my master Aristotle, if nothing else, at least the lesson he teaches of rational prudence; namely, that we must distrust any excess of simplicity in a philosophical statement about the *real.*

M. Bréhier's contention can be summed up in two or three simple theses; too simple, indeed, to be perfectly true to the complexity of human facts. He claims, first, that Greek systematic philosophy represents the whole of Hellenism; secondly, that Greek philosophy from Socrates to Plotinus is pure undiluted rationalism; finally, that there is strict identity between Greek thought and rationalism, exclusive of divine mystery.

The question we must ask is whether or not these contentions agree with what we can gather from the documents we have: inscriptions, poetry, drama, and history. What part did a truly religious spirit, the acknowledgement of a divine mystery and submission to it, play in the private and social life of the Greeks? What, for instance, was the *deisidaimonia,* that belief which St. Paul spoke of as a characteristic of the Athenian soul?

From a long and loving acquaintance with the classics, and especially with the poets, and Plato among the Philosophers, I had, in prewar days, come to the conclusion that the piety of the Greeks and their sense of the truly divine was genuine and deep, especially as expressed by their liturgy; that their religion was one thing and their corrupt mythology (which was never an object of faith for them) another. These ideas I treated in a little book entitled *La Piété Grecque.* A few years ago a similar subject was taken up and treated with much greater fulness and authority by Father Festugière, O.P., in his excellent book *L'Ideal Religieux des Grecs et L'Evangile.* For the following considerations on Greek Culture I am greatly indebted to the erudition of this eminent scholar and theologian, as well as to his sound appreciation and shrewd criticism of facts and theories.

HELLENIC CULTURE AND RATIONALISM

When St. Paul was preaching for the first time in Athens, Corinth, or Ephesus, was there anything in the make-up of his audience — in their education, their habits of mind, and systems of ethics and philosophy — which had prepared them for the message of Christ? Was there anything in the Gospel itself to answer and give satisfaction to the needs of the specifically Hellenic mind, as Greek institutions, traditions, and literature had formed that mind? Is there any truth in the idea that reasonableness, good manners, and the perfection of good taste are pagan virtues in the sense that they are opposed to Christianity, that they make men self-satisfied, enclose him in a sphere of human well-being, and shut him off from all perspective, hope, and desire of eternity?

If it is so, then St. Thomas (and before him the Fathers of the Church) was hopelessly mistaken, and in spite of himself, was at heart a pagan, when he converted into his own the Ethics of Aristotle — at least all its positive part. And yet I dare say that one can be a perfect gentleman, a Greek gentleman at that, without losing all hope of salvation. Manners make the man; they do not necessarily make the Christian. But Christian faith and Christian holiness perfect manners and the man.

Is it true to say that Greek paganism is synonymous with self-sufficiency, self-reliance, quiet pride, and a disposition to enjoy the happiness of a gently refined social life, in a mutual communication of pleasant thoughts and deeds? Is it, as Aeschylus puts it, *Xharmata antididoien?* But even did we accept this as true, could we say that such a paganism was happy? Francis Thompson would deny it. But he goes to the other extreme and makes the Greeks more sad and down-hearted than they really were.

Paganism, says he, needed the spirit of Christianity to make it joyful. And there is truth in what he says. But pagan sadness is not the whole truth about the ancient world, though it is part of the truth. There is that sadness, that sense of innate misery in the life of man, which crops up in almost all their writings. Theognis has a sentence which he gives as an old proverb, and which Sophocles will repeat in his turn in one of his finest choruses:

The best for man were not to have been born; the second

best, if by ill fate he has seen the day, is a speedy death and oblivion. — *Theognis* (425–428).

Not to have been born exceeds every reckoning. — *Sophocles.*[1]

And another piece of Greek wisdom with which we often meet, and which was considered Greek common sense about life and death, is the answer to the question: How can we judge of happiness? Only from the point of view of death. When we are no more, then our children or friends will decide whether we have been happy or not. And what for the Greeks was the most enviable fate? To do something good and pleasing to the gods, and then to die. To die young is a blessing of the gods and a reward, as the gods themselves showed in the death of those pious sons, Cleobis and Bito.[2]

Yes, there is a root of pessimism in the pagan soul, and they are saved from despair only by religion and trust in the goodness of a divine providence. The myths of Homer, all those human weaknesses and worse than weaknesses of the gods, manifest an evil propensity towards naturalism and the divinisation of all natural instincts. That, doubtless, is true. But not only are these myths not the whole of their religion; they are not even an essential part of it. The true spirit of religious paganism is to be looked for in the rule of worship, the liturgy of the sacrifices. And the Liturgy, their *lex orandi,* implies belief in the goodness and justice of the gods, in one divine goodness and justice, and even in the dogma of monotheism.

Polytheism does not exclude a confused sense of the One God by right of absolute goodness. "Behind the numerous gods we can usually discover a more general divinity, vaguer, but also more exalted, and often more ancient than the rest. Man has never been in doubt that the qualities of God are such as can belong only to one." One thing surely has never been in doubt, and with Socrates it was a truth of religious

---

[1] μὴ φῦναι τὸν ἅπαντα νικᾷ λόγον — *Oedipus Coloneus* (1224–1225).
[2] Herodotus, I, 81.

common sense; namely, the identity of the divine attributes Justice and Goodness. And by that is meant that there is no division in the divine will, no justice of one god opposed to the justice of another.

There is a great mystery about the gods, what they are, how they are divine, and what their real divine name is. The Greeks preserved about them, and about their most proper designation in human language, the tradition of their ancestors who were nearer the gods and so must have known better than they themselves could guess. But one thing is certain, and it is that, from the beginning to the end, this world was considered by them as governed by the same constant, unswerving, infallible divine Wisdom. It is that which Socrates asks that his hearers grant him as an evident truth. And it is readily and universally granted. In the words of Mr. Hocking:

> Even when man has many deities, they are addressed in turn [for the most part] as the all-powerful, the Lord of lords. A polytheism that is not in some sense a henotheism is yet to be discovered. The many gods have had their birth one by one, each one in turn a god, or rather an attempt at God. The gods must grow in number because the first god-shapes are too poor. Each god satisfies within the region of his own group of events; seems hero and superlative enough in his own province. But another province requires another figure of God. Hence we may say that polytheisms are galleries of aborted monotheisms; collections of god-figures each of which well intends to be all, but is incompetent. There is no such thing in [secular] history as a primitive monotheism; but there is a permanent singleness in the thought of deity which man forever departs from, through loyalty to the variety of deity's manifestations. Polytheism, then, has its right and richness in its acknowledgment of the omnipresence of divinity.[3]

Another name too readily and gratuitously given to the religion of the Ancients is *Naturalism,* the divinisation and worship of the many forces in nature. But such worship can

---

[3] *Meaning of God in Human Experience* (Yale University Press).

be interpreted in two different and directly opposite senses. It might mean, of course, that the Earth from which all living things have their birth and growth, the visible Sun, the Moon, the Rain, and the Winds are divine and are gods; and that our senses can perceive all that is divine in them. Or else it might mean that there is in the Earth, in the growing plants, in the life of the forest and in the winds, a hidden divine principle. *Rerum Deus tenax vigor* — God the sustaining of all things. God, indeed, is everywhere. In other words, things are not mere things, as our positive and materialistic age takes them to be; they are expressions of some divine power and will, and they deserve in their degree our respect and veneration. And the latter is more exactly the authentic ancient feeling.

Is there not, in such worship, a soul of genuine worship, akin to Franciscan and medieval piety? *Panta plere Theon*. The gods are everywhere. What does that mean?

When visitors were lingering with some hesitation on the threshold of Heraclitus' kitchen, the Philosopher called to them thus: "Come in; the gods are everywhere, and no less in my kitchen." And here Aristotle observes: "I too may say to those supercilious, fastidious creatures who find fault with my study of such vile and loathsome things as the lower animals: 'The God is here in these low objects as he is in heaven.'" Would that some of our modern naturalists had more of this pious naturalism of Aristotle.[4]

There is in nature about us a divine secret, such that it is not and never shall be wholly subject to our will. Yet at the same time it creates between man and the natural objects surrounding him a closer affinity and almost a brotherhood — although within varying degrees — by effecting a common participation in the divine principle. And these things are sacred, insofar as they are divinely ordained to help us in our life and in the fulfilment of a divine destiny.

When I myself was young, children in Catholic families

----

[4] Aristotle, *de Partibus Animalium,* I, 5.

were brought up in a sort of veneration of bread (an Eleusinian reminiscence!). Bread, they understood, should not be thrown away or wantonly wasted. It should be eaten with reverence and gratitude. Sorry indeed I should be to find this residue of pagan "superstition" dying away. It is far more Christian than Eleusinian.

But I shall not deny, for all these considerations, the existence of really superstitious aberrations and of a tendency — which is not specifically Hellenistic or pagan but simply human — to lower the divine to a level with our own weakness, instead of raising the hope and ambition of our weakness to the divine ideal. But I maintain that such superstition was not the whole, nor even the essence, of religion in the minds of the Greeks; for there was also in their religion a strong element of genuine *eusebeia,* that is, of real reverence and piety.

It is urged that the Greeks had no idea of what we call *sin,* or of the dealings of man, the sinner or the saint, with the justice or the mercy of God. In the life of man, as in the Whole, they are said to have considered only the necessity and eternal order of nature, without any divine initiative or intervention. In the words of M. Brèhier:

> Hellenic reason will not admit in things any beginning, any change that is spontaneous and imprevisible, such as Creation, the sin of man and Redemption. . . .

Drama is commonly accepted to be the form of art that is most expressive of popular ideas, traditions, ways of thinking and feeling. Yet in Greek drama, one thing seems to me to be evident; it is the haunting idea of man's injustice and of divine Justice interfering with the course of things to punish and reward. And the stress is on the punishment. Popular and poetic Hellenism is so much imbued with *deisidaimonia,* the fear of God and His judgement, that a system of philosophy has been invented partly to fight the widespread prejudice and to liberate man from the "idle" fear of the divinity.

Epicurus, a genuine *Graius homo,* was first, we are told, to be so bold as to rise against those depressing fears of thunder and lightning as heavenly signs of an irate divinity; he was the first to deny that there was in such natural phenomena the least divine intention or spontaneous will. That the Greeks had a living idea of *sin* and of absolute moral evil, the wilful breaking of an absolute and divine law, a law which is the same for Greek and barbarian, a law for all time and for all men; that they believed in God as the avenger of crime, can be proven by their historians, their art, and especially their drama. Such belief is the mainspring of the highest Greek tragedy, and as the tragedy was written and acted to be understood by the people and was moreover a popular function, it, if anything, is a reliable witness to the common belief.

There is a story, told of Themistocles, that on a certain day he had the brightest idea of his life. As the whole of the panhellenic fleet was moored at Pagasae, a wholesale fire of it, thought he, would be for Athens and her naval hegemony, the luckiest of accidents. And that accident could be very easily "managed." It was a grand idea, useful to the city, and its boldness and the thoroughness of the purpose made it pleasant to the aesthetic mind. It was, in a sense, "beautiful." Still, the Athenians felt some scruple about it and submitted the idea to the judgement of the "just" Aristides. "Indeed," said Aristides, "nothing more useful could be imagined; and nothing more unjust." The people would not burden their conscience with that injustice and the purpose was abandoned.

Be it fact or fiction, the tale is authentic and Greek, and it bears witness to the Greek ideas of the *just* as distinct from the *useful* or the *beautiful,* other than both, and of infinitely more value.

Here is another tale from Herodotus (vi, 86) about injustice and sins of the mind as being hateful to the God and punished by Him, even apart from the question of their actual execution.

The two sons of a wealthy Milesian who had been killed in a revolution, went to Sparta and presented themselves to the Spartan Glaucus, renowned everywhere in Greece for his justice, asking for a sum of money which their father had entrusted to Glaucus. They showed him the "symbol" of the trust, but Glaucus "did not remember." "Still," he said, "I shall go to Delphi to consult the oracle." He went to Delphi and here is the answer he received from the god:

> Glaucus, son of Epicydes, here is the course which is un-doubtedly the more profitable for the present: forswear thyself and keep the money. Forswear, since faithful or for-sworn, thou art equally fated to die. But the perjury begets an anonymous child, without hands or feet; yet it is swift, and it springs and cleaves to the perjuror's posterity till his house and race be utterly destroyed.

Glaucus then repented and said that he would give back the trust. But the Pythia answered that it amounted to the same thing to tempt the god and conceive the crime in one's mind, as to accomplish it in effect. Glaucus went back to his home in Sparta, called back the Milesians and gave them their trust. Still, in the present day there is to be found in Sparta no house, nor any man to keep alive the name of Glaucus.

"Hence you may conclude that in a matter of trust it is not even good to deliberate whether one shall keep his word or not." In that wise does the Spartan king Leutichydies conclude his tale when reminding the Athenians of a promise which they seemed to have forgotten. Sad to say, they were not moved to remember their oath, even by this edifying story.

But we are not concerned here with the practice of justice; what is in question now is the idea which the Greeks had of justice. And we find that with them Justice had a sacred and divine character; so divine, in fact, that *asebein* and *adikein,* godlessness and wickedness, were almost synonymous terms.

Aeschylus and Sophocles both have the same lesson to teach the people. May we not say that the chief purpose, or at

least one of the chief purposes of the Greek drama, is to
purify the idea of Nemesis by doing away with what was a
distorted image of divine retribution and putting in its place
a Nemesis that is more morally divine?

Nemesis, says Aeschylus, does not pursue excessive wealth
or a too constant human happiness, but only sin.

> It is an old and common proverb that when man has
> achieved the work of his fortune, his happiness is not bar-
> ren; its offspring is ever-unsated grief. I dare hold the con-
> trary opinion. It is impiety that begets woe, but justice is
> ever blessed with fruits of beauty.

Greek superstition tended to make the justice of the gods
awful, in proportion as it was unaccountable or less human
and more removed from our ideas of justice. The purpose of
Aeschylus is, in a sense, to humanise divine retribution in
bringing it nearer to what man conceives as absolute right
or wrong. And so it is quite true to say, as does Mr. A. W.
Benn; that "the Aeschylean drama shows us Greek religion
at the highest level it could reach unaided by philosophical
reflection." He adds that with Sophocles, "a perceptible decline has already begun." Instead of "decline" I should suggest
"regression," and that only in one or two of the earlier works.

The *Ajax,* for example, is a drama of the crude and inhuman Nemesis. But we must not find fault with this Nemesis,
is the poet's implication, for what are we to dispute with the
gods? We have only to submit ourselves to it. When Ajax
has been struck with madness by Athena, Ulysses is invited
by the goddess to join her in making sport of the hero's
degradation. But he will not do so. He feels too much, in
beholding the fate inflicted on his enemy, the condition of
his own human helplessness. What a poor thing is human
nature compared with the mysterious all-mastery of the gods!

> In sooth, I can but pity him, though he was my enemy;
> considering the curse that binds him all over, I see in his
> fate my own misery. For what are we, wretched men, while
> we live? Mere unsubstantial figures and fleeting shadows.

What could be more removed from that trust in human nature, that divinisation of man and man's reason, than such blind submission to an inscrutable and unavoidable Nemesis? It is a far way to rationalism indeed.

But the theology of Sophocles does not stop there. He is too religious to lower Deity to the human level. Like Aeschylus himself, he tries to raise mortal man to a closer affinity with the gods. In a sense we may say that he makes the god's will more human, more interested in Man's destiny. Nemesis is interpreted as Providence, whose ways, although mysterious, tend ultimately to the good of man.

The dramatic story of *Oedipus* might be summed up in the title "Oedipus in quest of his destiny." First he is a wanderer on the face of the earth, homeless and godless; then a lucky adventurer; then, a king, growing to the consciousness of his state. He would apparently be justified in thinking that now at last he has found the secret of his fate. But the revelation of the awful truth that through no conscious fault of his own he is under a curse, and is himself a curse to his city, drives him forth again, a hopeless wanderer. And it is then only, in his utmost misery, that he finds a divine answer and discovers that in the seeming curse there was a divine election and privilege. He has been raised to a higher level. In the sacred enclosure of the Eumenides, he finds himself at home. His trial has been a sort of consecration; he can deal with the gods more freely than the common people. His tomb will be a blessing to the land which owns it and a curse to the invader. Finally, answering the call, he dies, alone with the god.

That conclusion, it is true, does not leave our mind free from complexities. If it is meant as an answer to the riddle of the human responsibility of man's destiny, it is unsatisfactory. It is not the answer of a rationalistic humanist, of a man who believes in Man as master of his spiritual destiny, as sole captain of his soul. Rather it impresses upon us the Socratic and Platonic lesson that "God and not any man's thought or passing fancy, is the measure of all things."

To conclude, the mind, the common sense of the Greek, was religious and more inclined to superstitious fear than to human self-reliance. The work of the greatest and most popular representatives of Greek art seems to have been to raise that common sense to a higher and more religious level of optimistic trust in the gods.

Euripides, it is true, was a pessimist and a rationalist, but he had to disguise his rationalism under a veil of religious enthusiasm. And even so, public opinion held him, as it did Protagoras the humanist, and the sophists in general, under suspicion of the most grievous offence, that of impiety.

GREEK PHILOSOPHY AND RATIONALISM

First, let me remark that Greek philosophy cannot stand for the whole Hellenic culture. It is only an aspect and a part of it; and it so happens that the systems of the philosophers are at least partially conceived in opposition to widespread Hellenic beliefs. But even apart from that, is it true to say that, taken by itself and considered as an historical whole from Socrates to Plotinus, Greek philosophy is altogether rationalistic?

According to M. Bréhier, the Greek philosopher is wholly concerned with a perfectly rational *cosmos* in which there is no place for free divine intervention. That remains to be seen. I do not deny that there is a stream of "rationalism," in the narrow sense, running through that history; but I strongly deny that rationalism is the soul of Greek philosophy.

SOCRATES

Let us begin with the Father of Greek philosophical wisdom: Socrates. It is indeed true that he believes in Reason, and that that belief is at the source of his quest. The world and everything in it must be intelligible, he holds, and must fulfil the expectations of the intellect. It must be a *cosmos*, must exhibit a rational order.

But that *cosmos* is for him the realisation of some *good,* conceived and intended by a divine Mind. That there is on the whole and in the details a divine end or good in view, he fearlessly asserts. But once he has established that as a fundamental dogma, he does not pass his time in the contemplation of the celestial cosmos, nor does he incite his disciples to such contemplation. What is to him of supreme importance, as a thinker and as a God-inspired moralist (for he believes in a divine mission), is not the order of the heavens but the order in the human soul. Whether or not the individual man realises it, the fact remains that his supreme interest and his only care must be, with God's help to realise that order, to make his soul like God through the practice of virtue, justice, piety, temperance; in short, to save his soul. A rationalism, if you like, but slightly different from the one proposed by M. Bréhier as Greek rationalism. To look after our soul and to save it, that is the chief, the only business of the individual man, and he may, with the help of God, accomplish it.

But if by rationalism we are to understand the right and the power of human reason to explain adequately the physical, cosmos, the mystery of man, of his soul and his destiny, Socrates is decidedly not a rationalist. Here is his view: We know enough to save our souls and so to fulfil the will of God. As for God's ultimate intentions as to the destiny of man, we may make rational guesses about it, but finally it is God's secret. We believe in immortality and find arguments to prove it, but when all is rationally said and done, we can but trust the more probable and hopeful hypothesis, unless we get certitude from some divine revelation.

Such I take to be the meaning of the well-known passage from *Phaedo:*

> I feel myself (and I daresay that you have the same feeling), how hard or rather impossible is the attainment of any certainty about questions such as these in the present life. And yet I should deem him a coward who did not

prove what is said about them to the uttermost, or whose heart failed him before he had examined them on every side. For he should persevere until he has achieved one of two things: either he should discover, or be taught the truth about them; or, if this be impossible, I would have him take the best and most irrefragable of human theories, and let this be the raft upon which he sails through life — not without risk, as I admit, if he cannot find some word of God which will more surely and safely carry him.

This is the true Socrates. It is, of course, true that, being gifted with an exceptional power of dialectics, he is fond of reasoning and arguing, even to the point of being tiresome for the modern reader. And that passion for arguing may sometimes lead him astray, as in the Protagoras, and manifest a utilitarian view of Ethics. But that superficial eccentricity must not blind us to the fact of Socrates' deeply reverent and religious and almost mystic mind.

True, he did not believe in Mythology, but rather thought and taught that it was a corruption of the pure, traditional religion. He professed himself an agnostic as regards the very names of the God; an agnosticism which was rather a deep sense of the divine mystery. But he believed firmly in the dogmas which were implicitly asserted in the traditional liturgy; namely, that whatever be the name and the various manifestations of the Godhead, there is one divine Goodness, one divine Justice, one divine Providence. That belief was the soul of his "rationalism." It is for that Philosophy, penetrated through and through with reverent submission to the just and mysterious will of God, that Socrates lived and died.

Such, at any rate, is the Socrates whom Plato knew and loved. Let us now turn to Plato himself.

PLATO

Even supposing that Plato was mistaken about his master, if the passages in these Socratic Dialogues where there is question of the salvation of the soul by the practice of virtues, of the crimes which sully the soul with the marks of slavery, of the Divinity as the inexorable judge of both good and bad, do not express Socrates' own ideas, they certainly indicate the mind of Plato. And since Plato, at the age of more than eighty years, will repeat them with the same force, the same gravity, in "The Laws," we may well believe that we have here his doctrine on the matters in question.

But on the other hand, there is much else that might be said on the rationalism of Plato and the philosophical salvation which he proposes: It is a salvation that seems purely and entirely intellectual and contemplative, to be worked out apparently without the aid of "divine grace." The object of it is the *Idea* which philosophically is God, the perfect and beatific reality, but which gives no evidence of personal attributes of knowledge or of providence; and which is as far removed and divergent from any notion of human morality as the God of Spinoza. Father Festugière has written a chapter of pregnant criticism on this subject which might be the last word, were it but balanced by some compensatory reservations. The following is a résumé of what he has written:

In every system of philosophy one question is of prime importance, namely: What is the salvation promised therein? Perhaps we should rather ask: What "divine assimilation," what "divinisation" takes place in it? These are terms which even for the Epicurean are synonymous with salvation and happiness. What, then, is the salvation which Plato, the theorist of *Ideas,* promises us?

The divine, he tells us, is intelligible being. Immortality is the property of unchangeable being, of pure intelligibility, of the *Idea.* Man's spirit participates in immortality by his affinity with the Idea. Blessed immortality, then, will consist in contemplation. It is not the grace of a god. If Plato does not explicitly exclude grace, its utility, at least, is certainly not evident in his theory. The soul which is well inclined towards the Idea, which is attracted to the contemplation of it, has no need of grace. Moreover, the training necessary for this contemplation is entirely intellectual. Moral virtue is merely an indirect condition of the exercise of contemplation; it insures for the soul full liberty in casting aside everything which could possibly cause distraction. Indeed, according to Plato (and Plotinus), the soul is not sullied by vice; for the intellectual soul, the divine soul in us is Vision — power of vision; the faculty remains always the same and its keenness is not blunted. All that is required is to turn it in the right direction. The soul full of passions cannot contemplate the Idea, any more than it would have the leisure to be a good geometrician.

Of course, reasoning along the lines of this system, one ends by excluding divine help and grace as useless; but does Plato himself reason thus, and does he arrive at this conclusion? Does he anywhere say: "Man, thy salvation is within thee. Do not await in lazy fashion the co-operation of some unknown protecting divinity; expect nothing from the mysteries or from prayer. Exercise thy faculties; geometry will conduct thee to dialectics and after that thou wilt find 'the good' infallibly"?

Plato does not exactly say that, but what favours a rationalistic interpretation is perhaps equally as serious. He mistrusts inspiration and those who are inspired. The criticism of the poets in the *Republic* ought to be taken seriously, as also the avowal that the poets are inspired by some god and so are worthy of reproach and indulgence. They do not know what they are doing. Their inspiration, as he conceives of it, is infrarational like that of the seers. It belongs to the lower part of the soul, and it is that fact which condemns it in the eyes of the sage. It is a kind of obscure sensible wisdom which takes the place of the reason for the inferior part of the soul, deprived as it is of *logos* and *pheonesis,* of reason and practical common sense. Its seat and organ is the liver.

That this statement must be ascribed to him is undeniably true, but it would be very serious if it were the expression of the real and better Plato. Even more than a dialectician, he is a politician and a moralist. In politics he aims at the moral

welfare of the citizen and makes it depend on the worship of
the gods. As a moralist his idea is divine assimilation, by which
he means contemplation. But as for Socrates so with Plato himself, it is also the realisation of a divine work, of an image of
justice in the soul and in the state. And virtue here is not an
extrinsic condition but an integral part of the work. What is
more, all can aspire after it. Salvation is for all, just as the
judgement of souls is for all. For this divinisation we depend
on the gods; I do not say on the theoretical God of the Ideas,
but on the God and gods of the religion of Plato, which is
the traditional religion purged of the immoral myths.

There is no doubt that Plato claims that all virtue, for
whomsoever it be, may be reduced to the principle of right
thinking. Virtue remains knowledge or wisdom, and vice is
ignorance. But does it depend upon ourselves to think well?
Is not divine assistance thought to be useful and even necessary? There are as many texts in Plato which stress this dependence as there are texts to exalt reason alone, and I know
of no texts which deny it.

Because Plato makes light of divine help when it is directed
merely to the inferior, concupiscible, and carnal part of the
soul, it does not necessarily follow that he denies the possibility and the need of grace for the higher part, the mind and
spirit. The *Timeus* is here an eloquent witness:

"And now it is your turn to speak," said Socrates to Timeus,
after they had invoked the gods according to the custom. To
which Timeus replied,

"To be sure, Socrates. And every man, however lacking in
reason he may be, in every enterprise, be it great or small,
first invokes the gods. So much the more is it necessary for us,
as we are about to discuss whether this whole, which is the
universe, had a beginning or not, that under penalty of going
astray and losing ourselves we should before all things invoke
the gods and goddesses, asking them in our prayer that our
discourse may be in complete conformity with their spirit and
consistent with ourselves."

Moreover, Timeus, and Socrates, and Plato as well, agree
that on such a subject they can arrive only at what is probable; for such they consider to be the weakness of human
reason:

> We must be satisfied with the theory which seems most
> probable, remembering — both I who am speaking to you,
> and you who are the judges of my words — our condition as
> human beings, and thus demanding nothing on this subject
> beyond the probable.

As a matter of fact, it would be very difficult to make of
Plato a free-thinker, one who feels that he can dispense with
the divine. Nor can I conceive how anyone could express
himself more clearly than this Greek author does on what we
call "sin," and the divine chastisement of sin. Fully to illus-
trate this it would be necessary to quote the whole of the
tenth book of the *Laws,* and especially everything that Plato
says with regard to the second kind of atheism, which is the
negation of providence.

According to Plotinus, prayer has only a sort of magic
efficacy. The wise man who is in search of God does not pray.
He has need of nothing but his reason. And if we are to
believe M. Bréhier, Plotinus is strictly Platonic on this point.
To prove the statement we are referred to a passage from the
Laws on the uselessness of prayer. But in the text cited Plato
is condemning only the prayer of the impious man who tries
to make the gods accomplices in his crime by promising them
presents. Every true good, however, comes from God and we
have to ask Him for it. There is a text of Jamblicus which
records a Pythagorean maxim to the effect that all men are
fools who hope to find good for themselves any place else
than from the gods.

Every perfect gift comes to us from God. This is one of the
most certain dogmas of Platonic theology. He recommends
not only prayer, but even the use of expiatory rites for the
man who is obsessed by sacrilegious thoughts, so that he may
be delivered from them by the gods.

We would say to this unhappy man who is plagued by a wretched desire night and day, and incited to sacrilege: "My poor friend, that which is plaguing you so is not an evil which comes from men or from the gods (for from the gods there can come but good) but it is a goading of your flesh, inherited because of some ancient offence that has not been expiated. You must fight it with all the strength you can muster. And here is the way to combat it: when such thoughts come to you, go to the *expiatory rites,* present yourself as a suppliant at the altars of the titulary deities, the liberators. That's the first thing you must do." (*Laws,* 854.)

It would be hard to find anything less rationalistic than this quotation. And the same is true of the idea that man is a plaything of the gods, and that what is important in life is to play for them the game which they expect.

Nor is it a discouraged and disillusioned Plato whom we have here. He has lost nothing of his intellectual courage and fortitude, nor of his confidence in rational dialectics as a means of reducing the multiple to an essential unity. The members of the nocturnal council, those supreme judges of the city, are to be philosophers. But the very first dogma of philosophy, as of holiness, is that the measure of all things is not some man, nor is it a purely human reason, but rather God and the divine *Nous* (Mind).

I do not pretend to reconcile here in a perfect manner the Theology of the *Laws* with that of the *Republic;* to solve the problem of the relation of the Good to the Demiurge, or to the Divinity that is at once watchful and provident. I think that what I have said is sufficient to show that integral Platonism, Platonism as it really was lived, in no way excludes the idea of a divine intervention for salvation.

ARISTOTLE

The closest approach to M. Bréhier's definition of rationalism to be found in Greek thought, is perhaps that afforded by Aristotle; though even here there is no conscious exclu-

sion of a divine gift nor any hostility to grace. As a matter of
fact Aristotle never had the opportunity of thinking about
grace. Of all the Greek thinkers who inherited the Socratic
Wisdom, he is the least Socratic, in the sense that he is the
least preoccupied with the salvation of the soul. The problem
of happiness, which is the problem of all the schools of
thought after him, does not hold the first and dominant posi-
tion in his doctrine. The *Ethics* seems to be but a chapter,
albeit far and away the most important, in the history of living things. It is a study of that very interesting animal,
man, in relation to his end in life. We can even say that the
question of happiness has never had a vital importance for
Aristotle, the man. *Solvitur philosophando.* Philosophise and
be happy, as we might render this here. Intellectual activity
is so obviously the most agreeable, the freest, purest, and most
independent occupation of man!

Father Festugière tells us that Aristotle leads us to the
garden of Epicurus. But does he lead us even there? It seems
to me that he would find that garden rather sad. For in the
Epicurean effort to deny Providence, there is a prejudice
against the possible intrusion of the divine in our life, a
straining of the will, analogous to that of the Stoics. Aristotle
is serene and happy in a different manner. His God (the God
of the *Physica,* a necessary hypothesis to assure the unity of
the Universe) is the Prime Mover, and if one meditates on
his *diagoge,* the course of his existence, he is found to be
Thought, pure thought of his thought, the eternal contemplation of the eternally perfect Intelligible, that is to say, of
himself.

The impetus that comes from this Aristotelian God, or the
attraction of his perfection, sets in motion all the machinery
of the world. He himself ignores the world, the lower heavens,
the spheres and much less does he interest himself in the
lowly earth and man, even though that man be a philosopher
and contemplator.

But we can take his eternal beatitude as a model for our

own blessedness in time. It is in this sense only, Aristotle holds, that the estate of man can be said to be divine. For from the point of view of a divine law, and of a divine guarantee of that law, and of happiness, it is no more divine than the estate of the brute beast, of a stone or of the elements. Is it less divine than that of the stars and the spheres? Aristotle, like Plato, has a cosmological proof of the existence of God; like Plato also, and just as forcefully, he affirms his belief in finality, and a finality which is divine. But for Plato "good," in the true sense of the word, is moral good, that of a will in all things conformed to the laws laid down by the divine will. The good of the star is either obedience to that law properly speaking or at least it is analogous to that obedience. The model or standard of good, then, is moral good, which is revealed to us by conscience.

For Aristotle the contrary seems to be true. And that not through any desire to contradict his master on this point, but simply because in so doing he was following the leaning of his spirit, which is more curious than moral, more speculative than practical. For him the cosmological good, or perfection of circular movement, is the model of all good. That is good in earthly phenomena, in animal life, and in the life of man himself, which imitates this movement.

"The starry heavens over our head," said Kant, "are objects of ever-renewed wonder." Now, for Aristotle, the starry heavens are all the more wonderful, if not the more interesting, and whatever exists below the spheres, animal life and man's life, simply imitates, in its fashion, the infallible circular course of stars and planets. For Plato it is the reverse: the moral law of man is the *analogatum princeps* and reaches from man's conscience to the starry heavens.

Is Aristotle really and deliberately a rationalist? Let us rather say that he is a searcher; the most genial of the searching spirits. He is studious, contemplative, a worker, and one who enjoyed rational syntheses. In that, Descartes, whose principal object seems to be physics, resembles him closely. There

is this difference, that Descartes is also interested in the practical applications of science; but for the one and the other,
insofar as they are natural philosophers, God is required to
explain the visible world, its formation, and the laws of its
movement. Descartes excludes finality from his physics; Aristotle is a finalist, but his finality is not a moral one. Yet Descartes, in private life, was sincerely religious. And as for Aristotle, everything leads us to believe that he was religious in
the manner of most ordinary folk of his day, sincerely, seriously, but not excessively. In certain of his works, both of his
youth and of his full maturity, in the *De Partibus Animalium*
and the *De Coelo,* there is a religious sense of an omnipresent
divinity, a spirit of studious devotion, of admiration, we might
even say an adoration of the divine perfection. And nothing
in the rest of his works does away with this attitude.

I cannot discuss here in detail Jaeger's conclusions on this
point. Let it be said to the praise of this penetrating com-
mentator that he extracts from his documents, often quite
summary, all the substance that can possibly be drawn — and
then still more! One passage is particularly interesting, the
one in which he treats the distinction which Aristotle seems
to make or suggest between two sources of knowledge, namely,
reason and a divining presentiment, the intellectual instinct
of spontaneous affirmation; neither being esteemed as superior
or inferior to the other, but each rather aiding and confirm-
ing the other.

On the subject of the sources of our belief in God Jaeger
has this to say: "Aristotle realized fully that even the most
powerful logic could never achieve the irresistible force of
that profound conviction which comes to the soul by means of
inspired presentiment." He would have placed inspiration
above reasoning reason. He would have distinguished as
clearly as Kant or Schleiermacher between faith and rational
knowledge, and, it would seem, not at all with the idea of
disparaging faith. "God," he says in a fragment of the treatise
on prayer, "is Spirit, or above the Spirit." The intellectual

way then, is not the only way, nor is it the highest or surest.

Again, speaking of the *Mysteries*, Aristotle says: "The initiate are not asked to learn or apprehend anything by the understanding, but rather to feel and go through a sensible experience which should put them in the desired attitude, supposing that they are capable of such experience." Notice the fine distinction between *pathein* and *mathein*, to suffer and to learn. Perhaps the exegesis here is out of proportion with the brevity of the one isolated text. But we can say without the slightest fear that there is nothing, even in the later philosophy of Aristotle, which would contradict the idea of a spiritual instinct more divine than reason. Who has recognised more clearly than Aristotle the radical weakness of the human reason and the fact that that, which in itself is most intelligible, is for our human reason, at first the least intelligible? That which is divine is beyond me and out of my reach; the divine, that is to say the heavens and what is beyond them.

But that very important Aristotelian thesis of the eternity of the world, is it not in direct opposition to the idea of an absolute divinity? Yes, it is in opposition if it aims consciously at a denial of Creation, if it is affirmed with the intention of giving the divine its place in the universe and preventing any usurpation. Aristotle completely ignores creation, I admit, but are we to take this idea of the eternity of an uncreated world, independent of God even in its being, as a key piece in a system which is always gratuitously supposed to be perfectly bound together? It seems to me, on the contrary that the most Aristotelian thesis of all, that of Act and Potentiality and of the primacy of the Act, leads logically to the thesis of the Creation which Plato presents when in the *Timeus* he speaks of the world as "begotten"; when he makes the *Good* "the author of being and of knowing, and himself above them both" in the *Republic;* and when in the *Banquet* he insinuates the universal and operating presence of the Beautiful, which moreover remains independent of all that participates in it and which would remain the same even were there nothing else in the world.

Aristotle will have none of this generation of the world, but while weakening and enervating the causality of the *pure act* by this process, how does he manage to save his principle of the primacy of the Act?

Aristotelianism, we may say, or at least this very important part of it, in no way contradicts the possibility of a *Divine Liberty*, Creator of the universe. On the contrary it necessitates and demands it. If Aristotle fails to see this consequence, it is due perhaps to a deadening of his religious sensibilities.

I fail to see in him any desire to lessen the rights of the Divinity, any formal demand for nature to follow a rigorously rationalistic course. Not to see; to be subject, whether by nature or by force of habit, to a myopia in natural philosophy, is not the same thing as to make a deliberate act of denial, nor is it tantamount to taking the attitude of a free thinker.

So, to return to our original point, let us simply admit that this truly great man surprises and saddens us a bit by his distressing serenity and his almost complete lack of religious anxiety.

EPICURUS

The Epicurean is, in one sense, the most rationalistic of the Sages: he denies Providence in the name of atomistic science. On the other hand, it cannot be truly said that "his object is to discover the order of things or the *Cosmos*." He rejects the *Cosmos* as well as Providence; and although he finds that "the relation between order and reason is extremely great" and that the proper function of reason is to establish order or to find it, we might well say that the Epicurean is really antirationalistic. He is the Philosopher of *Chance,* and his object is entirely terrestrial and human: enjoyment, rest, and sleep.

There is much of the Epicurean in Keats; in lines such as these, for instance:

O, for a draught of vintage, that hath been
  Cool'd a long age in the deep-delved earth,
Tasting of Flora and the country green,
  Dance and Provencal song and sunburnt mirth!
O for a beaker full of the warm South,
  Full of the true, the blushful Hippocrene,
With beeded bubbles winking at the brim,
  And purple-stainèd mouth;
That I might drink, and leave the world unseen,
  And with thee fade away into the forest dim:

But what is the joy that he expects to find? It is only the absence of the cares and burdens of life:

Fade far away, dissolve, and quite forget
  What thou among the leaves hast never known,
The weariness, the fever and the fret
Here, where men sit and hear each other groan;
Where palsy shakes a few sad, last grey hairs,
  Where youth grows pale, and spectre-thin, and dies;
Where but to think is to be full of sorrow
And leaden-eyed despairs,
Where Beauty cannot keep her lustrous eyes,
  Or new love pine at them beyond tomorrow.

                                        — *Ode to a Nightingale*

We must not make Epicurus more sublime than he really is, or more solicitous for the dignity of reason. It is true that happiness for the Epicurean, as well as for Socrates, consists in likeness to the gods; Epicureanism is a rational method of making oneself like to the gods, *isotheon,* and as happy as the gods. And there is nothing easier. Living is in itself a pleasure, and he who would taste, without reflection, the pure joy of living, would be perfectly happy, just like a god! — or like an animal without reason. What, then, is the good of reason? Simply to raise us above vain hopes and fears which hinder our enjoyment. Man creates for himself the two great obstacles to his own happiness: one is the superstition of a provident, avenging deity which rules our destiny, and the other is the scientific idea of an immutable order of things, of a rational fatalism as depressing as the fear of the gods.

Must we then throw over all science and religion? No, but

let us rather purify them both by a better guided, less ambitious and wiser reason. We shall keep the rational explanation of the world given us by the old physicist Democritus, the theory of the chance meeting of atoms.

And now, what power can the gods have over us? They are made of atoms just as we are, albeit by a more fortunate meeting. Religion, properly understood, consists in giving them a cult of admiration and praise. All beauty can be praised, and the praise costs us nothing.

Furthermore, science is purified of its oppressive necessity by the seed of liberty which we recognise in the atom. We have reason, we have liberty. Nothing else is required in order to make that reckoning of pleasures which will assure our beatitude. And this reckoning is a purification, too. Turbulent, restless desires trouble us. The desire to know comes in this category. But these desires are by no means necessary. Let us then free ourselves from these vain and fruitless activities, and leave only the one, necessary, elementary, and peaceful desire, that of living physically, as long as we may; for we must not trouble ourselves about the future.

This rationalism which denies all divine grace is not, however, necessarily impious. It is not meant to be. The Epicurean recognises the gods and forms "pious opinions" of them. "Piously" he denies Providence, relieving the divinity of a care which is unworthy of it and which would spoil its happiness. For the characteristic proper to God is unchangeable beatitude. We must not implicate Him in our poor changing affairs and fortunes, our wretchedness and sorrows. It is a recurrence of that old belief that suffering is impure and that the gods abhor all contact with it.

To the Epicurean, piety means praising the gods for what they are, and wishing them well; acquiescing in the happiness which they have by a necessity of nature, but without expecting from them any communication of this divine good. Piety and wisdom do not consist, as Aristotle would seem to indicate, in the contemplation of the divine order in the heavens or on earth. The Epicurean turns his back on every philosophy of the *cosmos* or of an intentional order. This is the Greek rationalism which most thoroughly excludes divine intervention in human affairs and the one which is the least interested in the work of the reason, which is science. This just in passing, to recall that rationalism is a complex term, and that a reason which wishes to be self-sufficient and exclude the divine is not, by that fact, necessarily consistent with itself.

In view of this, what will be the attitude of the Epicurean at the proclamation of the good tidings of the Gospel? According to the strict doctrine, the decision is already made. If there is an unknown God, on principle the Epicurean expects nothing of Him. The message does not concern him. But in practice, the case is not the same. That rational pride which turns a deaf ear to all divine advances is, happily, rare. Some good souls, weak souls conscious of their weakness, were led astray by what Epicureanism promises and does not give; joy, a simple, humble joy like that of children, the very opposite of Stoic constraint. But Epicurean sloth is also forced and just as dreary as Stoic indifference. That spontaneous, effortless joy, that habit of joy, no longer of the child, but of the man who knows life and is not afraid to think of death, is a trait characteristic of the disciples of Paul; it resounds in the church of Priscilla and Aquila. The hedonist may well have asked these new Christians: "What on earth is this message which makes you always as happy as gods and which makes it possible for you to participate in the divine joy?"

STOICISM

Stoicism proclaims the sufficiency of human reason. Though more religious than Epicureanism, it is, perhaps, in its doctrine, more opposed to any intervention of a personal providence in the course of human affairs. Man must find his happiness in himself. It is unworthy to expect as a free gift of the divinity what is within the power of our liberty. Such an irra-

tional wish is even an offence against God, who is Reason.
The doctrine is the rationalisation of the religious sense.
Everything in the world is divine and everything is divine
reason. In submitting to that Reason we do not renounce our
own, for it is one and the same with our reason. The *Logos*
is immanent in our soul. It is an all-wise and all-powerful
reason which keeps everything in order. Thus all is for the
best. We must force ourselves to this optimism, which is
hindered by the imagination, by the foolish desires and the
passions which spring from the partial view which we have
of things. For, although our reason is divine and does not
differ from the universal *Logos,* its scope is limited. What is
aimed at here is a higher rationalism, which distrusts a reason
that can easily be led captive by the passions, so that we may
believe in the divine Reason instead. To believe in the rational goodness of the cosmos, after all, requires an act of faith.

"This world is good," says Bradley, summing up the doctrine. "It is the best of worlds, and each part of it is a necessary evil." Taine speaks more respectfully of it: the Stoic,
Marcus Aurelius, says he,

> . . . affirms only that the world is one, that an order of
> law governs it and that that order has the harmony of a
> reason. . . . Whence . . . all is well and all is beautiful.
> Who can harm that unique and creative nature, since there
> is nothing outside of it? Who could hinder its efforts, since
> there is no other effort than its own? What beauty does not
> pale in the presence of that inexhaustible, pacifying power
> whose measured effort brings constantly into light the eter-
> nal tide of creatures, and which is developed by both their
> flow and their shocks? Who would not feel penetrated with
> admiration and joy [??] at the sight of that mute, living
> will? I shall have but a single thought since there is but a
> single being. I shall go beyond the narrow necessity of my
> own person; I shall conceive the universal god of whom I
> am one of the members and I shall act in accordance with
> that conception. It is not I that he loves, but the whole. It
> is not one isolated person whom he has produced but a com-
> munity of men bound together by social instincts and by the
> possession of the same reason. It is not, then, my own

isolated being that I shall serve, but human society. — (*Nouvelle Essais de Crit. et d'Hist.*, p. 103.)

That is rather high-brow eloquence, though authentic nevertheless. It is Stoicism; only the unpersuasive fervour which animates it, is modern. It is also more pedantic and for that reason farther removed from Hellenic simplicity.

Marcus Aurelius is the gospel for us who have penetrated philosophy and the sciences. He says to the people of our culture what Jesus Christ said to the people, etc.

Such was not the style of Socrates or of Epictetus or of Marcus Aurelius. And neither is it the Stoicism which Epictetus or Cleanthes or Marcus Aurelius lived. Modern Stoicism reduces itself to the pride of being a reason in a world without reason. It denies liberty, it denies Providence, it denies goodness, it denies prayer. But Epictetus prayed to the gods, or the God, the divinity, as if it was a living goodness. His was a reason prouder than that of Socrates, a reason which wanted to refer everything to itself and which, on the other hand, submitted in spite of itself to a certain goodness and seemed to call for a divine *gift of grace*. Confronted with the message of Paul it had the choice of a reason without hope, or else the acceptance of the good tidings. On principle it was hostile to the tidings, yet it longed for them. On principle the Stoic was supposed to expect nothing from the divinity. On principle he denied the possibility of a divine gift or of a free message. To him, everything was divine, in the sense that everything was rational and rationally necessary. Reason might be adored in the world, or still better in oneself. One might admire and adore in silence. His adoration was still rational when the Stoic considered the limits of his individuality as contrasted with the universal *Logos*. But he had nothing to say other than that, "It is so." He had no wish to formulate, even less a favour to ask. And yet he prayed. In spite of his Stoicism the living Stoic could not get along without prayer. It is true that certain of the prayers he said were only the formula of the necessary acceptance of the inevitable:

> Lead me where thou wilst, O destiny; I am willing. And
> even did I not wish it, thou wilst lead me there just the
> same. — (*I. ab Arnim Stoicorum, Veterum Fragmenta.*)

But the famous hymn to Zeus has a more personal note. It
seems to go far beyond the law of universal reason to attain
to goodness, for it implores assistance for the weakness of
man. Though it lacks vigour, yet take away that piety which
rationalism must consider superstitious, and it is no longer
the prayer of Cleanthes; it is the most vain rhapsody:

> Glorious among the Immortals, God of many names,
> omnipotent forever; Zeus, master and guide of nature,
> sovereign legislator, I greet thee; for man has this power,
> this privilege, alone among living things, of naming thee,
> of addressing thee; for only we human beings are of thy
> race. . . . Wherefore shall I celebrate thee in my hymns; I
> shall sing thy might. . . .
> This world obeys thee as it turns around the Earth, sub-
> missive to thy power, to the thunder of the divine fire which
> thy invincible hand doth brandish. By it dost thou direct
> the universal reason spread everywhere, mingled in the
> heavens with the torches, great and small. (*Ibid.*, 537.)

So far that may be only eloquent myth and symbolism.
But the prayer continues:

> And on the earth also everything depends upon thee.
> Nothing is done without thee unless it be the evil which
> the wicked in their folly commit.

This certainly refers to the straying of the will which does
not enter into the divine plan; it refers to sin. It is true,
however, that Zeus will be able to draw good from error imputable to human folly:

> Thou puttest back in order what is awry, thou orderest
> what is in disorder, and what is not good thou regardest as
> good, or else thou dost transform it into goodness and from
> it drawest good.

Here one hesitates. The literal translation is: "what is not
good, what is not lovable [to us no doubt] is good and lovable

to thee." That would mean that there is no evil for the divine reason, for everything is foreseen and forms a part of the willed order. And that is, in fact, one of the explanations of evil given by the Stoic and the Neoplatonist: between good and evil there is nothing but a difference of viewpoint. For Zeus everything is good, just as good as good can be. Evil is relative to our ignorance of the whole. But Cleanthes has told us that bad actions are aside from the will of God:

> Thou hast so well harmonized things that there is for all only one eternal *Logos*. But the wicked turn away from it. Turned toward ambition, riches and voluptuousness, they do not understand that divine order, which to obey, is to be wise and to be happy.
> But O Zeus, master of every gift, save men from their foolishness and their lamentable ignorance.
> Pull aside from my soul this veil of ignorance. Grant to it to share in thy wisdom by which thou governest all, in order that we may return to thee honor for honor, giving to thy works perpetual praise; for there is not for mortals nor even for the gods themselves any higher privilege than to give fitting glory to the universal law. . . .

In spite of all, that prayer does not sound Christian. It is confused and disillusioning. There is an abyss between that acceptance of the law and the *Fiat voluntas tua* of the Gospel, the "Our Father . . . Thy will be done on earth . . .," where there is a will to be accomplished which has been given us to accomplish, where there is a divine work to be done freely with a freedom divinely aided, a work in which the omnipotence of God becomes man's helper. That was clearly suggested by Plato when he said that the gods are our helpers in our struggle for good against evil. But the Stoic does not think of this. He does not know what to think. He debates between his fatalism, which counsels inertia, and an irrepressible need of praying to a Father.

There you have a perplexed Stoic. But it does not befit a rationalist to be perplexed. He does not wonder if he ought to pray; that is spontaneous. But while he is invoking a goodness and a Providence, while he is imploring a grace, he wonders if the *Logos* of his system authorises that invocation, or if, according to strict Stoical logic, the only prayer ought to be an *"Amen* — it is so, and it cannot be otherwise," said to an impersonal and indifferent Fate, that is, without hate and without love. This perplexity is more manifest in Marcus Aurelius, who believes and does not believe in a meaning of things, and who wants to believe in it, at least in the possibility of giving a meaning to his own life, in the midst of the indifference of the *Cosmos* to what we call good or evil: "If all is in vain, be not thou in vain!"

Will it be said that this is to attribute gratuitously to the Greek the sentiment which is most contrary to Greek serenity, mental perturbation? What is not Greek is the romanticism of perturbation, uncertainty of heart cultivated as a distinction, or virtue of the soul, the maudlin enjoyment of being troubled. But what is simply human is the need of a motive, and a divine motive, for living, and the consciousness of man's inability to find that motive. That is the case of a clear mind which takes life seriously. The Greek has a clear mind, but is he serious? There is a prejudice to the effect that he is essentially frivolous. Nothing that is Greek prevents him from being serious, unless seriousness be confused with "Roman gravity," realism, or the Roman sense of realities. The Greeks were not serious in the same way as Cato the Elder; thank heaven!

In regard to conduct, logical Stoicism is much more opposed to the Greek genius. It is ascetical tension without any object other than itself, the sustained effort of not wishing: *Abstine et sustine,* "Abstain and bear up under it." The precept is required by the logic of the system; it is rational Stoicism. But the Greek genius does not support this melancholy any more than the drab "pleasure" of the Epicurean. The Hellenic mind is capable of inventing both systems; but to live them is something else. Socrates, who survives in both the Stoic and the Epicurean who sat as hearers before Paul, is not astonished at the unknown God and His message.

NEOPLATONISM

As a matter of fact, however, if Socrates survives authentically still in Plotinus, he has rejected the message of the Gospel. If Neoplatonism is the terminus of Greek philosophy, the case seems judged: reason has consciously set aside faith and the nonrational dogma of a divine adventure "into human history." Plotinus opposes deliberately (for he knows them) the Christian ideas of sin, divine grace, and the necessity of prayer. And this is all the more remarkable because his starting point is the experience of the "fall of the soul." But since Plotinus is in a way the most religious of the philosophers, and the heir of all the Hellenic philosophy, one is tempted to say that Hellenic wisdom and reason has its last say in him, and that apart from all supernatural assistance and by the powers of his spirit alone, it promises to man the liberation of the soul and the most perfect assimilation with God that can be conceived.

Prayer, according to Plotinus, can have for its object only earthly goods, and it has a certain magical efficacy by reason of a universal sympathy in nature. But the wise man has no need of it. His reason is more divine than all the *daimons*. By his reason alone he can promise himself to obtain the only good which he desires: his conversion and union with the One. In religions there are purifying rites, but the soul has no need of them to be purified. It is pure originally and cannot lose its purity. What keeps it far from its object is ignorance and a sensible cloak of ignorance; namely, the passions. Rational meditation, according to Platonistic dialectics, is the only means of freeing the soul from these exterior encumbrances and orienting it towards its divine object.

That is true, but the rationalism of Plotinus has, on its positive side, a special nature and perhaps carries its enemy within itself. Edward Caird opposes to the "Rationalism" of Plato the mysticism of Plotinus:

When we consider how Plato regarded the vision of the
poet and the prophet as, indeed, inspired, but an inspired
madness — in other words as a kind of intuitive perception
which could give no intelligible account of itself, and as
therefore far lower than the reflective insight of the philosopher, it seems absurd that Plotinus should appeal to
him, as the founder of a philosophy which maintains that
we approach nearest to the divine in an ecstatic state of
feeling in which all definite thought is lost. (*Evolution of
Theology in the Greek Philosophers,* II.)

I do not cite this text as definitive on the subject, but it
invites us to examine more closely the logic of Plotinianism,
its starting point and its conclusions. I find some antinomies
there; and the first of these I find in the exposition that M.
Bréhier himself makes of the system. The starting point and
fundamental reason for the whole system is the nonrational
feeling of a fall or disgrace of the soul — a point which bears
a strong resemblance to what the Christians call sin, and even
original sin — from which flows the necessity of a liberation, if
not a purification. And the positive explanation of that fall
is given in terms of sin: *tolma,* insolent audacity, the deliberate turning of the soul to what is beneath it instead of keeping
its gaze fixed upon the *Nous* (the Mind) and the Good from
which it proceeds. These may be symbolical expressions, even
mystical if you wish, because when we are at last united with
the One we see, according to this doctrine, the complete
necessity of everything which proceeds from It and realise
as a consequence, that the fall of the soul, its liberation and
its return, were only illusions.

But there is something more. The final step is just as far
beyond the reach of reason as was the beginning. Caird points
this out and M. Bréhier is not unaware of it: the Good is
above the *Nous* and above every effort of clear reason. Reason
has had no positive part in the soul's ascension, but has merely
brushed aside some obstacles. And finally, philosophic beatitude is not of the rational order but is a stranger to reason.
The Good itself must be freed of all rational necessity. What

Plotinus asserts most strongly is the liberty of the Good and first of all, the negative attribute of independence:

> We cannot say anything of It except that everything proceeds from It, as do all the attributes of excellence. But the cause is above that which it gives.

But to save that independence it is necessary to go farther.

The Good *is.* How is It? How is it that It is? We are forced to say: "We must stop here. It is because It is"; *sumbainei,* "It happens to be."

If we stop at a purely rational necessity, that necessity is inert and passively suffered. It might be said that the Good takes Itself as It is, as It cannot but be; just as for a king by right of birth royalty is a fact which he must accept. That does not satisfy Plotinus. And although every attribute is improper to It, that which he finally finds the least improper is that of will. It is because It wishes to be. It is the Good because It is the Will of good (*Enn.,* VI, 8).

I cannot develop these indications. It seems to me beyond doubt that Plotinian thought places at the top of things not reason and geometrical or suprageometrical necessity, but the Good and the Will of good, the Good which wills itself and which wills every good proceeding from itself. This is not far from creative liberty and love. It is not far from it, and at the same time it is very far away. What he says does not seem to come from a mystic sense of the love of God, but from the effort to define absolute independence. No matter. If he approaches thus closely the idea of a creative liberty, he is not diametrically opposed to the Christian dogma of a creation by love, of a Providence, of the activity of the will being exercised upon the world in an ineffable and unforeseeable way. He will not make that Divine activity dependent upon reason itself. If the liberty of God is snatched away from the control of reason, this is the greatest defeat of rationalism.

It would not be wise, however, by an obvious exaggeration to lose a good case. What a paradox, to speak of a creating love in connection with Plotinus! If it has been possible to

speak with reason of the love of God in that philosophy, it is
a love of the soul for God and a love which, just as the
amor intellectualis of Spinoza, does not and cannot expect
any reciprocity. That divine liberty of which Plotinus is so
jealous remains for him a negative attribute. The One wishes
freely and eternally its divine Unity; it cannot wish anything
else for it does not know anything else. The unfortunate
Aristotelian doctrine of a divine perfection of ignorance and
indifference, is perpetuated in Neoplatonism. Love looks up-
wards, as does cognition, and never beneath itself; or if it
does, there is a fall. The fall of the soul is explained in this
way by its love for the world beneath it and the pleasure
which it finds in it. Such a fall is unthinkable when there is
question of the One. It knows nothing beneath itself, not even
the *Nous* which proceeds immediately from itself.

But absolute indifference, although it can be understood of
the Aristotelian God, who is pure Thought of His thought,
fits in less well with the Will, which is, according to Plotinus,
the essential divine attribute, rather than thought. God is the
cause of the world by superabundance. Is it the superabundance of an impassible goodness or of a goodness which likes
to spread itself and which freely chooses to do so? If God is
Will, can His superabundance be anything else but voluntary?
It is characteristic of every excellence to overflow and in the
range of our experience it is called generosity or benevolence.
No doubt it is that also in the Cause of causes, but incompre-
hensibly. But it seems to me that this antinomy of the divine
generosity with the principle that the higher does not turn
towards the lower, is not insoluble. The higher can know
what proceeds from itself without turning away from itself
and without making itself dependent in any way upon the
lower object. The imperfection or fault which would cause a
fall would consist in submitting itself to the object, taking
satisfaction in it and forgetting itself in the contemplation
of the lower being.

I admit that Plotinus hardly speaks of that love. He leaves

us under the impression, rather, of a goodness without love. But the way is open. A free and wilful superabundance is admitted by Plotinus. The transition to the creating love is a logical step.

Proclus, a later disciple, answers the Plotinian objection about divine Providence, which he takes in the Platonistic and Christian sense, in this way:

> The divinity, it is said, cannot have the foreknowledge of sensible things because of the very excellence of his cognitive power. . . . But God knows everything in as much as He is the cause of everything in the depth of His thought and in the simplicity of His essence. Suppose that a man makes a ship and puts on board some passengers whose substance He himself sustains, and that, being master of the winds, he lets blow those which he wishes, as he wishes, without going outside of himself. In that case he knows from his own ideas everything that happens to the ship. Similarly but in a much more sublime fashion, the divine intelligence, which has in itself all causes at the same time, sustains everything in being and does this without going outside of itself, since immutability is the highest perfection of its essence. (*In Parmenidem,* V. p. 224.)

Proclus puts us on the right path, but it is reserved to Dionysius to give to the purified Neoplatonism its final and Christian expression:

> The good is the cause of all love. . . . It is for it and because of it that the inferior beings love the superior by turning towards them, that equals have for one another a love of communication of goods, that superior beings have, with respect to the inferior, a love of providence, and that each being loves itself with a love of conservation. The daring of truth will go as far as to say that He, Himself, the Cause of everything by the excess of His goodness, loves all things, loves with true love, and is intent upon all things, creating everything by that love, giving to everything His perfection, maintaining them in being and turning them towards Himself. . . . He is divine love, He is good with the goodness that comes from the Good. He is beneficent love for things which are, Himself subsisting infinitely in the Good. He did not wish the good to remain sterile; He has prompted it to operate according to the infinite efficacy of His virtue. (*Names of God,* IV, 10.)

Some people do not want to hear of a Christian philosophy, nor of the fusion of Hellenic thought and Christianity. But what shall we think of this beautiful text? All Christian mysticism, from the most humble to the most sublime degree, has lived on it and lives on it still. And yet it is Neoplatonistic, as is all the work of Dionysius, the disciple of Proclus. It is impossible to separate one element from the other; they are matter and form, soul and body. This is Plotinianism carried to a height at which Plotinus is dazzled and no longer recognises himself.

*　　*　　*

At the end of this chapter, already too long, I should resist the temptation of an apodictic summary. It is Mr. Bergson, however, who suggests it. He very rightly notes the mysticism at the origin and at the close of Greek philosophy. Socrates, the inspired follower of Pythagoras, expects a revelation from beyond the grave. At the close Plotinus exhorts us to put aside all reason and adore the mystery of divine Liberty. Mysticism is the inspiration of the Father of Rationalism! With the Neoplatonist, who fell heir to all wisdom, comes the defeat of reason and the triumph of Mysticism!

No, reason is not vanquished, and its long labor has not been in vain. But it does not, cannot go the whole way and the reason of the Greeks is too lucid not to admit sooner or later its impotency. It does not give the divine; and yet the need of the divine is at the bottom of the Hellenic soul. To the longing for divine happiness Socrates can only answer: "Wait for death," or ". . . if some God. . . ." But Paul says: "He for whom you are waiting, this God unknown and yet so near, This is it whom I announce to you." Christ says: "I am the Life." Greek reason has nothing to sacrifice in order to answer: "My Lord and my God!"

Incapable of making an entirely rational Divine being out of rational necessity, it must give up all hope of it, or else consent to accept it from a divine Liberty and Love.

CHAPTER TWO

THE RELIGION OF SPINOZA

SPINOZA IS PRESENTED TO US AS AN EXAMPLE OF a high religious consciousness. However debatable may be the dogma that he proposes to us, there is no doubt that he is a spiritual and a religious man, and he tends in his thought to lift our life above immediate interests, up to God; that is, if the word *God* is taken at least as a sort of symbol, as a guarantee of disinterested thought, or even as the principle of plenitude and purity of spiritual life.

We cannot help but ponder over the life of this man, who was so simple and yet so extraordinary in his proud simplicity; over his complete lack of any ambition other than that of right thinking, and of living according to that thinking. We recall that he was driven from the synagogue for having, among other "impieties," preferred the message of Jesus to that of the prophets. Friend of the De Witt brothers, counsellor of politicians and friend of the common people in whose midst he lived, living as they lived by means of his trade, he was jealous only of the independence of his thought. *C'était un homme doux, Benoit de Spinoza,* says the French poet; the most modest of men, the boldest of thinkers, and a singularly attractive figure.

Though barred from the synagogue for his unorthodox tendencies, he would go neither to a Catholic nor a Protestant church; but when his host's children returned from the meeting house on Sundays, he always made them repeat for him the sermons they had just heard. Was he an atheist, one of those peaceful and mild atheists one sometimes meets with? No, the testimony of those in whose midst he lived would never permit us to believe that. But we must look for the real Spinoza, the interior man, there where we find him talking, as it were to himself; namely, in that studied prose where, reckless geometrician, he would define the Absolute, its attributes and modes, God and man and the passions of man, in rigorously mathematical terms, *more geometrico*.

Let us glance back over a few revealing pages: the prologue of the *De Emendatione,* the conclusion of the *Ethica,* the heroic end that he proposes for himself and the accomplishment of that end, liberty and immortality gained through spiritual love:

> The end: the search for a sovereign Good; that is to say, of a nature such that it is above time and change, the enjoyment of which is eternal [recall the words of the Gospel: "A treasure in heaven which faileth not: where no thief approacheth nor moth currupteth"]; that is the supreme good and perfect liberty.
>
> If such a Good exists [and that to him is still uncertain], in order to attempt the attainment of a Good which is perhaps illusory, must we break loose from the ordinary good things which incite our appetite and ambition? Must we leave the prey at hand for the shadow? Or shall we more prudently begin the quest without renouncing anything of that which we love? No, that is impossible. This one unique good claims all our effort; we must choose between the common goods at our immediate beck and call, and the risk to be run in pursuing this unique Good. But the choice is already made; we have already experienced the futility of common goods.
>
> The advantage of this sovereign good of the spirit is that it cannot be the occasion of discord among men. It does not divide men, like appetite or avarice; rather, it unites them.

In the last analysis — according to Spinoza's course of thought — that immortal good which is eternal life, is the knowledge of divine ideas, or the participation in the divine idea which represents such and such a particular transitory

essence under the aspect of eternity. The spirit of man is then
no longer bound up with the mortality of this world; it becomes rather the eternal view of it. The insight into the real
meaning of the world is for Spinoza love of God, a pure love
which does not look for any recompense. We need not expect
a return of love on the part of God, argues Spinoza, but as a
matter of fact such a return of love is a necessity. With the
same love with which God loves Himself infinitely, He loves
also all that proceeds from Himself *sub specie aeternitatis*,
"under the aspect of eternity." He loves this thought which
rejoins His thought, which identifies itself with His. This love
is singular, as is the knowledge itself; for the divine ideas are
not universals, those false ideas of Aristotle, as Spinoza considers them, but ideas of singular "modes." Thus the wise
man, perfectly freed from his passions in the adequate idea
that he has of God, in the direct knowledge of the "modes"
such as they proceed from God, and in the spiritual love
which he has for God, sees himself as he is, directly loved by
God. But this beatitude does not depend on our own effort.
We do not gain liberty by an illusory "free will"; but we
can wish for and finally possess the Good. ("It is not of him
that willeth, nor of him that runneth, but of God that show-
eth mercy" — Rom. 9:16.) He who attains this summit of
knowledge, this state of pure love, can consider himself the
object of a great privilege and a divine grace.

This God of the liberating spirit, continues Spinoza, who is
Liberty and Love; this God, whose reign is in us, has been
revealed by Jesus. Jesus has brought us real salvation. The
prophets talked only figuratively; the salvation they an-
nounced was a salvation of obedience, not of liberty. We must
not search for this beatitude in mercenary things. We must
practise piety, religion, grandeur of soul and generosity, for
themselves. This virtue in its highest degree constitutes happiness. Beatitude is not a reward for virtue, but the virtue
itself. And it is entirely gratuitous. We are not given it for
having conquered our concupiscence, but we are masters of

our passions because we have beatitude or in the measure in which we approach it. The ignorant man is at the mercy of external causes. He can never possess real peace, and living, so to speak, entirely ignorant of himself, of the things around him and of God, he ceases to exist at the moment that he ceases to suffer. The wise man, on the contrary, is hardly ever bothered by any passion, but being fully conscious of God, of himself, and of the things about him, he never ceases to exist but is assured of real peace for all time. Such is the conclusion of the philosophy of Spinoza. Between it and the beginning, the grave announcement of the undertaking, we have the history, or rather geometrical account, of man's servitude and of his progress towards liberty.

THE SPINOZAN DOCTRINE

The doctrine presents an appearance of unity and coherence, and the connection between the "ethics" and religion appears to be as clear as one could philosophically desire. The starting point is from the order of ethics. It is a search after the real good, conceived beforehand by anticipation as something eternal and divine. However, the point of view is human. That for which man is searching is a state of happiness; he cannot be indifferent to happiness. But he has already renounced his riches, his pleasure and vanity, all the transitory goods which can deceive the heart of man made for eternity. His destination is divine, the knowledge and love of God and union with God. That is beatitude. Thus the wisdom which prompted me to search for the real good was, equivalently, it might be claimed, religion, a need of God, the searching after God.

Still, if we look more closely, the question is not so very clear or simple. I can see very well a desire for happiness and its fulfilment finally in beatitude, but religion is something else. It is the service of God and love of God before we possess Him. When is it that the Spinozan man is, properly speaking, religious? The starting point of his ethics is eudemonistic, not religious; it ignores God, or at least it can ignore Him. It has nothing to do with the idea of a Good above all other good or of an eternal happiness. The divine in this case might be nothing more than an epithet of excellence. The definition of God does not call for any sort of real cult; it is a mere affair of geometric reasoning. The same is true of the deductions as to the world, man, and his passions. Reason alone is sovereign; doubtless the philosopher hypostatises it — identifies it with God — but man does not owe it any other cult than that of right reasoning. There is no need for prayer. As for the ethics, they follow quite necessarily and naturally, without my ever having to know that this reason is the Divine Reason, the Substance, God. All is reasoning, or, as for that which has to do with conduct, Epicurean wisdom of foresight and calculation. The idea of the divine is at the very end of this philosophy, but then religion, or that which is commonly meant by the term, is left aside. We are invited to a state of ecstasy. The whole is a strange continuity, from a wisdom altogether earthly to the most abstract mysticism.

What is there in this man's work which is so captivating, which gives the impression of a God-inebriate soul, and even of religion in its perfect purity? And that, too, despite the dryness of the deductions, the austerity of certain conclusions which should shock our religious sensibilities! For after all, it is in one sense, a religion of absolute divine insensibility. Perhaps it is just that which appeals to us; the contrast between the fervour and ardour of hope of the soul in quest of the divine and of divine happiness, and the inexorable severity of philosophical and theological reason, the generosity of the enterprise, the glorious risk that is run, the ascetic renunciation as a condition of the spiritual future. Then, too, there is the implacable probity of a reason which does not wish to find delight save in truth, without regard for moral sensibility.

Without doubt, it would be more agreeable for us to fashion a God more according to our preconceived notions, favourable

to our enterprise, accessible to our prayers; a God after our
own heart, in other words; and a sort of world where our
free will might exercise some freedom, a world of values which
might be at the same time human and realisable by effort and
human liberty, and divine and absolute as well. But reason,
Spinoza argues, will never prompt us to do anything like
that. It forbids us to disparage divinity thus in attributing to
it ideas and wills which could have the slightest analogy to
our own. The first thing we must do is to follow our reason
— and in following reason it is God Himself we are presumed
to be following! We must accept the truth, whether it be
flattering or cruel, simply because it is the truth.

What is man for Spinoza? A mode of extension, a system of
precarious movements, but animated by an effort to persevere
in being, *conatus, in suo esse perseverandi,* a will to live. We
must understand by that the individual man, not the Scholastic
notion of man in general, the sublime and for Spinoza quite
vain idea of humanity with its privileged dignity of divine
idea. Nothing for him is real save concrete facts of movements
in space. And for the supergeometrician or the substantial
geometry which is God, one movement has exactly the same
value as another, which is no value at all; for our categories
of good and evil are only relative to human interest and have
no sense in the mind of God.

Salvation and happiness, in this system, do not in the least
concern divinity. From the point of view of God, everything
in the world is said to be good, at all times, just as it is; that
is, if one wishes to give the name of "Goodness" to the divine
geometric necessity. This indifference of heaven may discour-
age a weak soul, but not the hero of Thought. And who
would not wish to be a hero? We were warned at the outset
by Spinoza himself that the adventure; namely, the philosophical quest for the Good, was for heroes only and required
heroic resolve and perseverance. Carry on, search for the truth
for the sake of truth, not for yourself. Search for God for the
sake of God; there is no other prize, no other recompense but

Truth, but God. Love this God with a love that does not devolve into self-love, for this religion realises (it is the only one which does realise) love that is spiritual, absolute, and absolutely disinterested.

Such is Spinoza's religion, as he presents it. It is for him more than religion. It is the summit of mysticism, ecstasy, and absorption in God. It is true that in this utter abandon of love, the soul finds itself, but divinised, if you will. It realises, he is ready to promise it, immortality above all that which passes, above an infinite duration of time; it realises more than immortality — eternity.

By an admirable paradox, this wisdom unites an Epicurean candour and frank admission of human values, traced to their strictly human source, and a Stoic heroism. This wise man wanted nothing but truth for its own sake; he loved truth for truth's sake; hard, dismal, indifferent truth. But what he was not searching for, what he forbade himself to search for, that he believes he finds in the end, and a hundredfold; love of God for Himself. More than love, in fact: perfect unanimity, union, and unity. Escaping from the transient modes, he settles himself and possesses himself *sub specie aeternitatis*.

I have made this résumé as plausible and persuasive as possible, giving merely the general scheme, blurring over the inconsistencies; and I have done it with the vibration of the grand words and immortal sentences still lingering and sounding in my memory, half conquered by the austere eloquence, subdued by all the more contagious emotion. But now we must examine with cold reasoning the sense and rational value of this Spinozan emotion. I am afraid there is more feeling and imagination in this divine intoxication that is so contagious, than there is of reason. With the same rational vigour which Spinoza pretends to use in establishing divine indifference concerning human values, the illusory character of human free will, etc., let us in our turn examine, according to the texts, the axioms and the definitions, and finally the religious value of this religion. We do not wish to be duped

by eloquence, even if it be the eloquence of Spinoza. "Geometric eloquence" is perhaps the most misleading of all.

Let us go back to the beginning and read an important
passage of the *De Intellectus Emendatione*. Only we must
beware of allowing ourselves to be impressed by the lofty and
at the same time discreetly emotional tone of the style.

From love of perishable things spring quarrels, disputes,
envy and fear. We must then renounce these things in order
to adhere to eternal goods alone. Love of an object that is
eternal and infinite fills the soul with pure joy and frees it
from all sadness. Nevertheless all the time that my mind was
occupied with these thoughts, I could feel nothing but aver-
sion for these transitory things. These intervals of meditation were rare and short-lived at first, but in the measure
that I entered deeper and deeper into the knowledge of the
Good, I meditated and thought on it more often and for
longer periods. And this especially when I discovered that
the pursuit of riches, pleasure and honors was harmful if
these things were sought for themselves, but not if one only
wished to make use of them as a means to attain a higher
end. In the latter case there could no longer be any fear
of abuse, and in place of doing harm, these creatures could
do great good.

I shall set down here that which I mean by true good
and what I mean by the "sovereign good." But, to avoid
confusion, let it be known that good and evil are purely
relative terms, so much so that one object can at one and
the same time, be said to be good or bad, according to its
various aspects. And the same is true of imperfect and perfect. For nothing is by nature perfect or imperfect, especially when we consider that nothing takes place save in
compliance with an eternal order and the fixed laws of
nature. But our human weakness prevents us from ap-
prehending that order, and still, man conceives an ideal of
human nature, a sort of human nature more lasting than
are individuals; and seeing no opposition to the acquisition
of that nature, he feels himself constrained to search for the
means of attaining this perfection. Every means that is
helpful towards attaining the end is called a real good; the
sovereign good is to arrive at the enjoyment of such a perfection of nature and to bring other individuals to the same
enjoyment. We shall show later and more at length what
this nature is. Suffice it to say here that it is the knowledge,
the consciousness of the union which exists between our

mind and the whole of human nature. It is towards that that I am tending, to acquire such a nature and to bring it about in some manner or other that many others may acquire it with me.

Let me note in passing one rather important point in the doctrine, and that is the wisdom or prudence that tempers the renouncement of temporal goods. There is no need that this abandon be absolute; Diogenes, and still less the Christian ascetic, should not be our model here. True, we should not seek riches, pleasure, and glory as ends in themselves; but they can be very good as means. Health helps for wisdom, and money does wisdom no harm provided the intention be purified.

We must take Spinoza as he is and as he wishes to be. There is in his doctrine as a whole, a basis, which he believes solid, of utilitarian Epicureanism. He means to remain always reasonably attached in principle to worldly goods. But that which arrests my attention especially, is the undisguised avowal of an illusion in the very beginning. I am seeking a sovereign good; but what is that good? It is a relative end that is entirely human, and in no way divine. And the supreme good that I have proposed as my object? It also, for Spinoza, is relative to an illusion; it is the idea of a type of human perfection, the illusion of Scholastic realism which believes in the value of general ideas, whereas in a good philosophy of clear ideas, there is assumed to be nothing but individuals, or individual, concrete facts; and there is no idea to which we can refer these individuals to determine their value. The value of an individual could come only from a decree of divine predilection. But God, according to Spinoza, does not love; or, what comes to the same thing, the love of God makes no distinction between the various modes, this mode which is an ant and that other which is Socrates or Baruch de Spinoza, between an anthill and the Dutch Republic.

But one might answer to that objection: "What does the imaginary character of the ideal matter, if, applying to the quest the exactitude and probity of my reason, in the end I break loose from all illusion and attain God?" It is the end, the final result, and what Spinoza calls "intellectual love" of God, that we must examine, to see if it has even the faintest analogy with what is commonly called "love," or even with the definition of love previously given by Spinoza.

Love is defined as joy with the idea of the cause — joy at my growth in being, at my knowledge and my power; and the cause is God. Joy, then, supposes a tendency, a desire and a growth that follows the desire; it is a passion among other passions.

How are we to understand this extension of joy to the cause of the joy? As a matter of fact, I love him who does good to me, provided he really wishes to do me good. Love responds to love, the will to do good to the will to do good. Just an idea of cause accompanying joy is not love. For instance, a timely rain is the cause of the desired fecundity of my field. I am glad for it. I love, if you will, the cause of this growth. Is it with this love that I love God?

I shall love God, with that which can really be called "love," if God is the voluntary, loving cause; if God is interested in me. But how can I love pure indifference? Yet this pure indifference is a characteristic of the God of Spinoza. If He is not the creative love of which my love, itself also creative in its own degree, is a distant echo, if He is not the incomprehensible infinity of a Goodness, the resemblance of which I carry in myself, then I cannot attribute love to Him without taking away the real meaning of love. And I cannot bring myself to return a love which is inexistent and even self-contradictory. It is absurd that Spinoza's God should experience the passion of joy as defined by Spinoza, absurd that He should recognise anything as the cause of that growth.

Let us admit that we can find in the idea of this divinity — unacquainted with any value, with good or evil, infinitely transcending human values and devoid of all that I call good — a sort of religious horror, of ecstasy and a sense of divine liberation; the feeling of getting away from, of transcending time and the temporal, space and everything, even whatever exists in the realms of the spiritual which can remind us of these limits of time and space, the sense of entering at last into a Nothingness which is eternity.

Call it mysticism if you will. And one might very easily become ensnared by it, perpetuating the illusion by nourishing it with impressions and canticles of Neoplatonician and even Christian mysticism. But if this philosophy ends in beatitude, in the mysticism of divine Nothingness, I fail to see how we can any longer call it meditation or contemplation of life, or how it can establish a system of ethics, or what reason it can give me for action. Granting the possibility of Spinozist mysticism, there is no possibility of founding on it a system of ethics.

Any system of human progress, individual and social, under divine approbation and guidance, implies the Aristotelian theory of Act and Potency, which is in direct opposition to Spinozism. From the divine point of view, where intellectual love finds its center, the world is conceived by Spinoza as perfect at every instant; at every moment it is God, and it would be unholy to conceive a "progress" of God. God thus becomes the negation of every realisable ideal. Good and evil in the Spinozan philosophy, have no sense for divinity; nor have vice, virtue, justice, and injustice. It is necessary to repeat this, for the admirers, nay worshippers of Spinoza, always forget it!

It will be sufficient to quote here one of the most significant of the texts. It is the "Reply to Blyenburgh" (*Epistola* XIX *olim* XXXII). How can you reconcile, asks Blyenburgh, divine causality with moral evil and the sin of Adam? Spinoza replies: Nothing is more inaccurate than this term "sin," an offence against God, contrary to the will of God:

> I cannot grant that sins and evil are anything positive, much less that anything exists or is done against the will of God. I claim that only improperly or speaking in a human

way can we say that we commit sin against God, as when we say that men offend God.

The sin of Adam, the will to eat the forbidden fruit, insofar as it is real, is in Spinoza's doctrine entirely good; it is only wrong — i.e., what we call "wrong" — in comparison with other more perfect realities. Its rightness or wrongness is entirely relative, and the proof of that relativity is that we admire in animals what we disapprove in man; jealousy, for instance, and its effects. A will contrary to the will of God? To speak of the will of Adam as evil because it is in opposition to the will of God is as contradictory for Spinoza as to speak of a square circle, for that which would be in opposition to the divine will would be in opposition to the divine intelligence as well. Where is the evil? Only in the privation that should follow. And here again, continues Spinoza, it is privation merely from our point of view, not from the divine point of view. Privation is a term which follows our conception of nature, the standard of perfection to which we refer all the individuals of a given species. We say then, that Adam has forfeited the privilege of a higher value. But the Spinozan God does not understand these abstractions; these universal terms are entirely relative to our intellects (or rather, our ignorance). He knows only particular things which have exactly the perfection of their creation. A human ideal, ideal of humanity or of any essence, is not a divine idea, but a purely human one.

If objection be made from Scripture, Spinoza replies: The Scriptures, the prophets and prophecy are adapted to the people. Divine causality is interpreted as a law which binds like human laws; the salvation of some and the damnation of others, which are necessary results of divine causality, are interpreted as recompense and punishment.

The difference between the good and the wicked boils down to a difference of degrees in the participation in the divine perfection. The former perform the will of God knowing the cause; the others fulfil it without knowing it.

ETHICS OF THE SPINOZAN RELIGION

Let us now examine the Ethics of this religion. There is in Spinozism a preliminary and purely provisional ethics, an ethics of the conditions of the search for God, which consists in the renouncement of all ambition and of all the cares and pleasures which might prove a hindrance to the mind and retard its flight. Abstinence is imposed in the measure in which it is necessary to keep a clear head and to be able to follow the chain of clear ideas. But that is nothing more than a point of mental hygiene which every student must observe. And furthermore the renouncement is not final, as we have already seen. Far from prohibiting the use of the goods of this world, Spinoza contents himself with repeating the golden rule: *ne quid nimis,* moderation in all things.

But besides this preliminary ethics, there is also a system of ethics which is an integral part of the religion; in fact there are two Spinozan ethics, and even a third (if indeed, having arrived at the summit of the experience of spiritual love, it is possible to impose a rule of life); this third would be the ethics of the generous-hearted, the great souls.

The first ethics, the most immediate and consequently, most divine, is that of pure nature. The second, the ethics of the wise man, is derived from the first and retains its principle, but it modifies its applications according to the conditions of society and also in accordance with the wisdom which follows from the knowledge of the second stage, the rational knowledge of the necessity of the modes. The following is a résumé of the sixteenth chapter of the *Theologico-Politicus* treatise:

> The right of nature extends as far as the power of nature, and its power is the power of God Himself. Each individual has a sovereign right over all that is in his power. The law of nature for every being is to persevere in being, disregarding all obstacles. And from this point of view there is no difference between men and beasts, between men endowed

with reason and those who know nothing of true reason. Just as the wise man has a sovereign right to do that which his reason commands, so also the ignorant man has the natural right to follow all the promptings of his appetite. Natural law, then, is defined by the desire of power. The ignorant are no more bound to live in compliance with the laws of a healthful soul than the cat is to follow the natural laws of the lion.

(It is well to note that these terms of health and even reason bear a necessary relation to a certain idea of human good. I would even go so far as to say that they imply a value of the universal concept and in particular of the concept "man," in direct opposition to the radical nominalism of Spinoza. Health is the state of normal man; reason is the knowledge that man, as man, has of human good. But what can that mean, when there is nothing but individuals and individual cases, each one of which is divine by the same right?)

Natural law, then may be defined as the individual's right to procure for himself all that his reason or his passions suggest to him as useful, and the right to procure this by any possible means: ruse, force or petition; considering as one's worst enemy whoever dares try to impede the attainment of it. But the desire to persevere in being implies a desire of security. And it is impossible to establish this security if each one is to be allowed to do as he pleases. Hence the necessary desire for union among men.

By this union, or contract of union, the individual transfers the right which he holds by nature to the organised group and henceforth it is the organised power and the will of all together and not the individual appetite which determines the rights of the individual.

(This transfer of rights, then, is merely a transfer of power. The state retains full rights over the individual because, and only as long as, it remains the stronger.)

The soundness of the pact depends on certain conditions, the chief of which is that the contract holds only insofar as, and as long as, it is considered useful. A useless pact ceases automatically to be binding. It is foolishness for a man to ask another to bind himself to a pact for all eternity, unless he can first see to it that the breaking of that pact will entail greater harm than good for him who breaks it. The guarantee of the social pact is the force of the state. He has a sovereign right whose power is sovereign. The state retains its right only so long as it retains its power.

The sovereign, whether it be a tyrant or the people, is not bound by any law. [He makes the law for all and imposes an ethics of the second degree.] The only guarantee against the abuse of absolute power is the sovereign's own interest in keeping himself in power. For he must know that a violent rule cannot last.

Whatever type of state there may be,

civil law is determined by the decisions of the sovereign power. The sovereign, being above all law, can never be said to violate a law. Between states there exists no other law than the purely natural law of force and appetite. If a contract is drawn up between confederated states, its only guarantee is its utility. It is against piety and religion to keep promises to the detriment of the state.

Everyone who lives outside the city is an enemy of the city. It is not hate which distinguishes an enemy, but the right which the state has against him and which he does not recognize. Neutrality has no meaning. Whoever does not adhere to the state is to be regarded in exactly the same light as one who does actual harm to it, and the state has exactly the same rights against him as against avowed enemies. It may force him into submission or compel him to become an ally.

The only crime against the state is the *vain attempt* to usurp the rights of the sovereign. If the crime is not nipped in the bud, and succeeds, the state, losing its power, shall lose also its right. (Sedition is punishable only insofar as it does not succeed; if it does succeed, it proves its right.)

That is the divine law of nature, as Spinoza sees it, and all that survives of it after man's "reason" has established together with society, laws and duties. The end is still the same; it is still the attainment of the supreme good, which is for each man to persevere, to sustain himself in being. Wisdom consists simply in the choice of the means. It must not be forgotten that in the eyes of God human society, according to this philosophy, is a mere fact of nature, "modal," just as the bee-

hive or the anthill, and of no more importance; the same is
true for internal wars, the bloody revolutions, coming from
within the society or the state. And since in all wars, inter-
national and civil, there is no arbiter between the two parties
either on earth or in heaven, the reason of the stronger prevails. Success, whether it be due to force or trickery, creates
right. Spinoza is not trying to be subversive; we do not repeat
all this in a spirit of indignation. His idea is simply to present
the rational history of the nature of man and of society, as he
conceives it, for the use of such learned men as will know
how to utilize it to the benefit of the majority of men.

Spinoza's own personal ethics, his personal attitude towards
men and things, bears no taint of this primitive law of appetite and violence, though he makes no secret of his intention to get the most out of nature's goods. The knowledge of
the second stage, the science of causes and effects and their
necessity, of man's precarious state in the infinite and necessary series of modes, delivers man from servility to his passions. The passions, fear, hope, hatred, irrational love, are
for Spinoza, all due to ignorance of natural necessities. Once
we have realised that our free will has nothing to do with
what we must undergo, be it pleasant or otherwise, we no
longer hate or hope, or are deceived or angered. For in the
words of Euripides, and of Marcus Aurelius after him: "Why
be angry with things, since it does them not the slightest
harm?" And this is the keynote of the conclusion of the fourth
part of the *Ethica:*

> Human power is always very limited and is infinitely in-
> ferior to that of external causes. Consequently we may not
> adapt to our own usage things which by their nature are
> beyond our control. But we shall bear with equanimity
> whatever happens to us if we feel that we have done our
> duty, and if we realize our powerlessness to do more and
> also the fact that we are but a small part of nature, whose
> order we must follow. Once these truths are clearly under-
> stood, that part of us which is defined by our intellect, the
> noblest part of our being, will have no difficulty in accept-

ing this order of nature and will make every effort to persevere in its acquiescence.

Acquiescentia: peace, repose, assent, and acceptation. Spinozan ethics, at this stage, is entirely independent of any consideration of eternity. It looks only to utility in this present life. It supposes the knowledge of God, but not, it would seem, intellectual love, if we are to understand by this a love springing from an intuition of the divine, distinct from the rational knowledge of pure necessity.

We must not permit the fact that the words, and in particular the word *Religion,* are used with various meanings, to confuse in our minds two things so different as the religion and the ethics of Spinoza. The ethics is the wisdom of the second degree, or stage, of knowledge; it is not a liberation, but the knowledge of necessity, and consequently alleviation of necessary servitude and acceptation of the necessity, once it is known. It is not, however, wholly negative. Positively, it helps us make this world more habitable, and life more tolerable. But once we set our hand to better society, we must be prepared to see our efforts frustrated. Success depends on us only in an infinitesimal degree. Virtue then, is still, for the most part, resignation.

From absolute rationalism, Spinoza can deduce a system of ethics. But that ethics does not free him and it has no religious meaning. It is simply utilitarian. Reason can only help us to recognise the conditions of happiness or of the peaceful enjoyment of the goods which nature provides, or else the best way of adapting ourselves to a servitude which is necessary and unavoidable. And the first way of doing this is to know that servitude. We might say that this knowledge frees us, not from the essential servitude created by my infinite dependence as regards the modes, but from the voluntary servitude to the passions which comes from ignorance. The universe may crush me, but I shall show no anger against it. To this knowledge of physical and divine necessity is added a positive

means of adapting oneself to the necessary servitude; it is that
of society, the communication of the goods of the soul. But
let us bear well in mind that this ethics has no divine meaning.
It aims at the enjoyment of nothing more than the goods that
this earth gives, without any thought of an afterlife. And on
the other hand, the religion or the mysticism of spiritual love
has no moral sense. The intellectual love of God is not the
same thing as love of one's neighbor. The one great Commandment of Christ is unknown, or rather, ignored.

This ethics of Spinoza, purely human, and in no way divine,
the simple intelligent prevision of enjoyment, is little better
than Epicurean atheism. The principle is precisely the same
in both, the self-maintaining impulse, the effort to persevere
in one's being; an individual effort, every man for himself.
His wise man sees no philosophical reason for creating a reality beyond and outside of himself, to be an object of devotion.
The state is nothing more to him than a means of realising
more surely his personal salvation. Unlike Kant, he has no
respect for humanity as such, nor is there any reason in his
philosophy why he should. Still less should he allow himself
to be deceived by a disinterested love of "man," for "man" is
an empty abstraction. There are no such things as essences
and natures. There are only individuals.

But the wise man of Spinoza's philosophy observes that war-
ring passions limit the precarious power of the individual,
while on the other hand, union and the sacrifice of appetite
to the common good bring about an increase of power for the
individual. There is no other reason than this for being generous, liberal, and without envy. Nothing is more helpful to
man in his struggle to persevere in his being and to assure for
himself the enjoyment of a rational life than to be guided by
reason in all things. For men who are animated by envy or
hate are sure to conflict with one another, and are the more
to be feared in proportion as they are stronger. Still, it is not
violence, but love and generosity that wins men's hearts.
(*Animi non armis, sed amore et generositate vincuntur.*) But

we must not forget that love is also a passion — and a sign of ignorance.

It is highly useful for men to form alliances among themselves to establish a unity out of their multiplicity, and to do all they can to strengthen this mutual friendship.

Benign, liberal, unambitious, and free from envy, the "wise" man's power is, finally, the most effective of all. In order that all may think in accordance with his generous reason, it is to his own interest to share his wisdom with others. But he is driven by no ulterior motive, no ambition of giving his name to a sect. He seeks merely that rational good which enslaves none but which is increased and perfected by the participation of all.

In reality, though, this wisdom is never more than a mere calculation. The best of calculations, to be sure, but never sure of its effect. The Spinozan wise man has no power to free others; he is never perfectly free himself. That which he calls liberty is the knowledge of his own servitude, and the resignation consequent to that knowledge.

WHITHER BOUND?

The *Short Treatise* of Spinoza is quite another story. Here the keynote is humility and courage and an enthusiasm which is almost evangelical, together with love of God and love of our neighbor. Here, finally, is an ethics of life and action. But is it rational? That is the important question.

He retains man's state of absolute dependence, to be sure, but it is now dependence on God. We are the servants and slaves of God, but for our own greater good, for to serve God is to reign. We depend on everything, but this everything is God, the most perfect being. We are a part of God and so we participate in the accomplishment of innumerable works, all marvelously ordered and perfect, which depend on God. Our servitude, from this point of view, is really participation in the sovereign power of God.

We must not fall victims of pride, however, Spinoza warns us, over the good that we have been able to accomplish, for such self-complacency would be contrary to the idea of our perfection, which consists in our duty of striving constantly to make further progress. We must recognise that God is the cause of all that we do, and this knowledge by fostering in us true love of our neighbor, does away with all hatred and anger and leaves in their places a desire to help him. (No more hatred or anger, doubtless; but what reasons are we given for positive love, other than reasons of personal selfish interest?)

We learn not to fear God, for how can we fear Him who is the sovereign Good? We learn to attribute everything to Him and to love Him alone because He is most excellent and most perfect, and thus we come to immolate ourselves entirely to Him. For it is therein that the real cult of God essentially consists, as well as our eternal salvation and beatitude.

All these ideas set forth by Spinoza would be very fine and beautiful, if only they were logical. But we must not forget that the idea of progress is merely human and inadequate, that it rather leads us back again to the enslavement of our passions, giving us the idea of doing better, with the illusion that it depends upon us to do better. And all this talk of the perfection of God and His works has not even an analogous meaning and can have no connection in Spinoza's philosophy with any human ideas of perfection, order, and beauty.

This *Short Treatise* can be meant, then, only for one who is but on the threshold of the beatitude and spiritual love which correspond to the knowledge of the Spinozan third degree. Once we have arrived at the summit, if we still have any illusions about acting in such a way as to do better each time, we must get rid of them. From the point of view of God and the love He has for us, the human individual has no more value than an earthworm. All his actions are indifferent; His crimes have the same approbation from God as his virtues. Everything is divine, and we should never permit any consideration of human interests to induce us to establish degrees in the divine. The knowledge of God may be beatitude, but it is inert. Supreme wisdom no longer consists in meditating on life. Such is the culmination of this philosophy. What Renan says of Marcus Aurelius holds good also, and with even greater reason, for the conclusion of the *Ethica*. It is an ethics of absolute ennui; "Wisdom was absolute, that is to say, that its tedium was limitless." The most solid goodness is that which is founded on absolute ennui and on the fact that every fact and everything in the world is frivolous and without any solid depth or meaning.

In brief, from the divine point of view, all is necessary in Spinoza's philosophy and all is perfect at every moment; or better still, nothing is more or less perfect at one moment than at another. There is no difference of value between beings and their actions. From the divine point of view, there is no reason for actions. The force of the ethics proposed will always be an illusion of value, or of possible progress to be made. If the former, then there is no moral dynamism in Spinozism; if the latter, his ethics is human and in no way divine.

It is hard to resign oneself to admit the final defeat of this fine effort at wisdom, of this doctrine of salvation that is so persuasive in its accent, its sincerity, and its fervour. Perhaps the technical logic is here merely a convenient, but very imperfect, cloak of a deeper thought and an intuition that is truer than the system. M. Bergson attempts to define the Spinozan intuition in the following words:

> It is the perception of a coincidence between the act by which the mind knows the truth perfectly, and the operation by which God engenders it; the idea that the conversion of the Alexandrians, when it becomes complete, becomes one with the emergence and that when a man, having emerged from the divinity, finally returns to it, he perceives but one unique movement where before he had seen the two inverse movements of going and returning; the moral experience here resolves a logical contradiction and by an abrupt suppression of time, makes of the return a going.

The intuition, then, would be an identification of the

created mind with the Creator and with creation. But just what is this moral experience peculiar to Spinoza, and how does it resolve the logical contradictions? With the Alexandrians the identification might consist in coincidence with a creative principle which is ineffable and inconceivable, but nevertheless, more analogous to a divine will than to mathematical cogitation; coincidence with a Good that wills itself and its fecundity, is diffusive of itself, truly creative, and as it were, absolutely free and above all rational mathematical necessity; creative and lavish with its creative gift. And the coincidence of our mind with Him would mean participation in that creative generosity and the will to make a new world.

I can very well see in this idea the basis for a lofty and rich ethics in both the human and divine, the social and the private order. But it is so because this intuition is realistic, creative, and optimistic. The world is good because it comes from God. It is good if I work to make it good, for my creative collaboration has been foreseen and willed by God.

But this God who *wills* a cosmic good, which is also the good of man and my good, and which I can understand since my divine destiny is to accomplish it, is diametrically opposed to the God of the *Ethica,* a creator of a cosmic geometry where everything is good since it is eternally necessary, where nothing is good of that which man calls good, or evil which man calls evil. Nowhere in the *Ethica* can I find that joy of creating, but only the joy (it pleases him to call it that) of knowing — from the point of view of eternity and of a divine outlook — the worthlessness of all human value.

We cannot enter here into the attempt of M. Delbos to inject a human and divine finality into a system whose very principle would seem to be the negation of all finality. If, further, we find in Spinoza some idea or feeling of a divine dynamism, of a Divine which desires to realise itself in the world and which demands our co-operation, we can be sure that it is outside of and in spite of the *Ethica.*

Asceticism, love of solitude, absolute independence, the

asceticism of geometric reason and the joy which is the recompense of that asceticism, all that may be called religion, and it undoubtedly has some of the characters of religion. The effort to persevere in one's being might well be the basis for a religion of progressive divinisation. And the call of God and the answer to that call is also religion. But it seems to me impossible, as well as decidedly unphilosophical, to try on the one hand to identify and to appreciate the fervour of the independent, laicised reason, purged of all divine transcendence and of any anthropomorphic interpretation of the divine, that is to say of any ethical value of the divine, and on the other hand to embrace at the same time the religion of a divine ideal which our nature is to realise, starting from the instinctive effort to persevere in being.

Marcus Aurelius, who made no pretensions of following a system, could well say: "If all is in vain, be thou not in vain!" But that is not, and could not be, the meaning of Spinoza when he says: "All is in vain from the point of view of God, that is to say, whatever end you propose to realise in this world, whatever good you desire, God knows nothing of it and He is God precisely because He ignores it. Divine indifference! Let us give it its true name: Eternal Reason, Divine Reason. We must contemplate it; it is adorable. And we must break away from the pursuance of any ideal or goal that our imagination, in its ignorance, sets before us."

All is in vain, and you are also in vain; rejoice that you are divinely in vain! Imitate, nay more, identify yourself with divine indifference! Renounce for the sake of God, and out of love for reason, which is God, all human happiness, the object of whatever human desire, even though, by a sort of impiety, one might call that happiness divine.

And what of Intellectual Love? There is not the slightest analogy between this spiritual love of the fifth book of the *Ethica* and all we understand by the word *love*. In the rigour of the system, the one has no more relation to the other than the constellation *Dog Star* has to a barking dog in the street.

And yet, for all that, we do not doubt the sincerity of Spinoza. We do not deny that there is in him a piety in the true sense of the word, a positive love that resembles our own love, the response to a divine love that watches over us and calls to us ever. But then, this God, is He still the God of pure reason, the God who belongs exclusively to the philosophers and scientists, and not the God of Abraham for whom the excommunicated Spinoza retains in his heart a nostalgic love and piety?

If the Intellectual Love is to have any meaning for us, we must say with Mr. Taylor:

> "If Spinoza was led by his own recommendation to the *amor intellectualis* the manifest reason is to be found, not in his philosophy, but in his personality. Like more than one great philosopher, he clearly had a personal religion which finds no adequate expression in his own professed metaphysic. The source of his actual piety towards God and the happiness it brought him is not to be found in the doctrine of *Deus-substantia* expounded in the First Part of the *Ethics;* we have to look for it in the deep impressions of early life based on intimate membership of a Jewish family and a Jewish community, familiar with the utterances of psalmists and prophets who most emphatically did not identify *Deus* and *Natura*."[1]

There is something of the God of Abraham and Isaac in the God of Spinoza, just as there is something of the God of the scientists and philosophers. And so, when Spinoza comes to pray in his heart (and I like to think that that was quite often), it is not the God of the philosophers that he addresses, but the God of the patriarchs and prophets; and since he places Christ above all men, he uses the prayer that Christ taught men, the Our Father. But if the Philosopher in him comes to the fore and begins to translate and transpose, there remains neither God, nor Father, nor Intellectual Love, but only the pride of the mind which takes itself for its God; the religion of pure Rationalism.

----

[1] *Faith of a Moralist* (Macmillan).

CHAPTER THREE

BERTRAND RUSSELL'S RELIGION WITHOUT GOD

THERE HAVE BEEN MANY ATTEMPTS, IN THE history of English thought, at a Religion without God, or, what comes to the same, with a finite God, the creature of man's brain and a mere symbol of his religious need. We shall here consider two modern instances: first that of Bertrand Russell, to whom the present chapter is devoted, and next that of his fellow Englishman, H. G. Wells, who is dealt with in the following chapter. I have selected these two authors not because of any special philosophical value in their conceptions, but because of the influence they enjoy in the popular world of letters.

We have at least two published essays by Bertrand Russell on the subject of godless religion and each admits of different interpretations. What they have in common is the "scientific" assumption (or shall we say "conclusion"?) that there is no divine thought that governs the Universe, that it is altogether purposeless and meaningless.

"If everything be in vain, be thou not in vain" are the words previously quoted here from the good emperor Marcus Aurelius. They were spoken by him in the dark moments when his creed of stoic optimism failed him. Mr. Bertrand Russell is more affirmative: for him everything *is* in vain. The Whole, of which man is an infinitesimal part, is even less rational than a bad joke; it is bare absurdity. It gives us nothing to care about, no hope, no human interest, no reason whatever why we should enjoy life and persevere in existence. How then, in that universe entirely devoid of meaning, are we to give a practical and religious meaning to our life? Is it necessary? Can't we comfortably "live in vain" without any troublesome, hopeless reflexion on the meaning or the vanity of living — follow the hedonistic impulse, enjoy or endure the instant? It does not seem possible to Mr. Russell. He at least needs some *raison de vivre* beyond the immediate interest, and he writes for those who experience the same need, who want to expand and devote their life to some object beyond self and the precarious limits of individual existence. Such devotion seems to be the essence of religion. It is "worship." But what shall be the "Free Man's Worship"?[1] "Free" here means free with a rational freedom, liberation from all irrational dogma or belief in God. How, then, without God, shall we preserve the ennobling, comforting, uplifting effect of worship?

In a previous essay on "Logic and Mysticism" the same writer sought to show that wisdom, or the spiritual perfection of man, is made up of two heterogeneous elements: first, science, the pure science of facts, expressed and measured mathematically, excluding all consideration of good or bad; and secondly, mysticism, the mental attitude which finds or imagines an object of love or worship beyond or outside the world of scientific analysis (which is for him the entirety of the real world). Unfortunately, however, there is a distressing discrepancy between his different definitions of the mystic sense.

At one time we are told that it is a *vision*. Its object would then be merely a postulate, not indeed of science, but of the scientific method. To analytic reason things would be neither good nor bad, to the mystic insight they would reveal a most real goodness and beauty. In the words of Browning, "the

----

[1] *Mysticism and Logic* (Allen and Unwin, London).

rest (the scientist) may reason, and welcome; 'tis we musicians (mystics) know."

But then, again, we are told that after all it is not so; the mystic sight does not mean knowledge of any kind. It is a *feeling*. "The mystic emotion reveals nothing about the world, it reveals a possibility of human nature."

Is this mystic sight or emotion, then, a wise and welcome illusion? Not at all; we must be loyal to reason and keep on all things the steady, clear gaze of science. Beware of believing in the reality of any actual good or of looking forward to the realisation of an external good.

Such belief, comforting as it may seem to the faint-hearted, would spoil both the sincerity of science and the pure disinterestedness of the mystic sense. That purity of mysticism goes so far as to exclude all consideration of what we call ethically good. Its object is "a good, foreign to our ethical ideas of good and evil." For mysticism is contemplative; it has nothing to do with action. "It overcomes the ethical dualism which action requires." Still more strange to say, in that wilful ignorance of the ethical point of view lies, for the mystic soul, the secret of an "ethical advance."

All that, at least to my unscientific mind, is perplexing enough. Let us, then, try to find a clearer and more coherent idea of Mr. Russell's religion in the two essays: "The Freeman's Worship," and "The Essence of Religion." In both essays the absolute meaninglessness of the universe is clearly asserted and firmly maintained throughout.

THE FREEMAN'S WORSHIP

"The Freeman's Worship" begins with a long quotation from Goethe's *Faust*. It is the description by Mephistopheles of Creation's monstrous absurdity. To this Bertrand Russell adds his own gloss to the effect that the world, which science presents to our belief, is even more purposeless, more devoid of meaning.

Into such a hopeless world, then, man is born with his sense
of right and wrong, his ideals; man, the clearsighted child of
blind Nature able to judge the absurd whole of which he is a
mere accidental product. For man, with his fears and hopes,
his loves and beliefs, "is but the outcome of accidental col-
location of atoms," part of the universal absurdity. But even
when he is scientifically aware of all this, he at least means to
live, and religion, worship, love of something other than the
immediate facts of experience, something deeper, higher, remains to him a vital need.

There existed in the beginning and for ages, and even now
exists for certain highly civilised people, we are told, a religion of servile fear. Its God is the overwhelming oppressive
power of Nature personified, a will of unlimited power which
can be made favourable by intercession and by prayer and
by worship. But as the moral sense gets stronger and more
imperative, man needs must find a worthier object of worship
and he imagines an ideal of goodness allied to power, a good
God, moral but *unreal.*

When we have realised that power is largely bad, that man
with his knowledge of good and evil is but a helpless atom in
a world which has no sufficient knowledge, the choice is again
presented to us: Shall we worship force or shall we worship
Goodness? Shall our God exist and be evil, or shall he be
recognised as the creation of our own conscience?

The Freeman's answer is obvious. Strength is good, by
all means let us have strength of mind, but not the brute
strength of a blind Nature, indifferent or hostile to all our
ideals; let us have moral strength, the power of resisting the
might that is bad, of denying its divine character.

"In this lies Man's true freedom, in the determination to
worship only the God created by our own love of the good."

Here is a clear answer: since there is no goodness in the
Universe, our God will be good but unreal, the God of our
moral ideal of goodness. What, then, shall be our attitude
towards the world of facts, the world as an object of science

— unconscious, blind, immoral? Shall it be ". . . to defy with Promethean constancy, a hostile universe"?

No, says Russell, for "indignation is still a bondage." It is a sort of homage paid to the Power we defy. It keeps our minds and hearts occupied with it. Let us submit to the necessary fact and forget it. Christian resignation is better than the pride of the rebel. Yet such silent submission is not religion, but opens the way to it. Only when we have heroically given up all selfish desire, made total sacrifice of self, and so conquered spiritual freedom, can we think of building a temple of the spirit and worship in it the unreal God made of our purest and noblest thoughts. But here one might object: the very stuff out of which our thoughts are made are the visions and the impression of the real and, therefore, the supposedly bad universe. True, but we possess the wonderful power of our mind to "transform and refashion the unconscious universe."

In this way the mind asserts its subtle mastery over the thoughtless forces of Nature. . . . The more evil the material with which it deals, the prouder our victory, the more triumphant the tragedy we make out of it.

Tragedy! The word brings with it a remarkable change in the Freeman's attitude toward religion. Instead of wilfully ignoring the world, cherishing and worshipping our secret ideal of goodness, we may contemplate the Whole and in it man, his conscience striving after some ideal good and carrying on its hopeless struggle with the overpowering forces of blind Nature. That dramatic Whole will be our object of thought. An object of tragic awe, but is not awe and the sense of the awful the characteristic of the religious feeling?

In itself the Whole is indeed meaningless, but considered as including the hopeless conflict of man's whole conscience and moral ambition with the blind forces of Nature, it becomes tragic. It has the awful and sacred character of tragedy. A disinterested contemplation of it is at the same time a liberation from all our petty cares about our existence.

We know that tragedy was in Greece part of the national Liturgy, a religious function; and we may admit that for the Greek the tragic sense was akin to the religious sense. But how was the poet to achieve that result of an emotion both dramatic and religious? Not by the representation of the vain struggle of man with Fate, both blind and impotent. Euripides did that, but Euripides' mind and intentions were the reverse of religious. On the contrary, tragedy tried to show in a spectacle of human woe the final triumph of some divine goodness. Its theme was the dealings of a divine and loving Providence with man's life. Sometimes, too often he failed to do so, the poet preferred to be accounted *tragikotatos* rather than *eusebestatos,* most tragic rather than most pious. But it would not be difficult to show that the trend of Aeschylus' and Sophocles' thought, in the *Oresteia* and in *Oedipus,* was religiously optimistic. They raised the tragedy to the level of religious emotion. Bertrand Russell does exactly the opposite, debasing religion to the level of mere tragic emotion.

Certainly the spectacle of the world is for him one of absolute and universal human wretchedness. Of what avail, he asks, are human virtues, lofty ideals against the immensity of the "Powers of Darkness"? But on the other hand it is not clear in what the tragic emotion consists, or just how it is religious.

> All the loneliness of humanity amid hostile forces is concentrated upon the individual soul which must struggle alone against the whole weight of a universe that cares nothing for his hopes and fears.

In this description, permit me to remark, there is a more or less deliberate illusion and self-deception regarding the supposed hostility, and wilful malignity of the Universe. Is it not a tacit confession that there exists in man the religious need of some living and omniscient God, be He good or bad? If the Universe, "the Whole," is simply insensible, lifeless, indifferent, there is no question of tragedy, but only of despair. What feeling can man rationally entertain towards brute, inanimate forces? Anger, indignation, are equally irrational. Euripides admirably expresses this idea in his humorous, pithy iambics:

It is useless to get angry with things; they don't care.

and with equally Euripidean common sense he gives the sane advice:

Try to make the best use of them; that is wisdom.

But what of Bertrand Russell? Unfortunately, as he proceeds he waxes more effusive than articulate. He suggests various ways of feeling religiously about things. At the same time he is not clear at all about the *object* of our worship. First he tells us to face things squarely, or to eye our fate in the midst of things, then it appears that the knowledge we shall thus acquire will be freedom, and I suppose, religion too:

To take into the inmost shrine of the soul the irresistible forces whose puppets we seem to be, death, and change, the irrevocableness of the past, and the powerlessness of man before the blind hurry of the universe from vanity to vanity; to feel those things and *know* them, is to *conquer* them.

To know oneself conquered and past all hope, is to conquer! That may be so if, instead of worshipping the forces of nature with servile fear, we admire their beauty, or the beauty of fate, or the tragic beauty of being so miserable ourselves.

The slave is doomed to worship Time and Fate and Death because they are greater than anything he finds in himself. But, great as they are, to think of them greatly, to feel their passionless splendour, is greater still.

There is, then, a grandeur in that insensibility and absurdity of things. Let us admire them; such absolutely disinterested admiration is freedom, and is religious worship as well. Better still, let us embrace and love and lose ourselves and all our selfish interests in that love. I suppose that is the sense of the following passage: "to abandon the struggle for private happiness — to burn with passion for eternal things [the latter having to do merely with human and earthly things]."

There is for him no God. All that makes the worth of life — thought and love — are in man alone. Let him then make to himself a God of that deaf and dumb and blind nature, or give her a tribute of praise and admiration as if she were a god. It may be freedom in a certain sense, liberation from fear, yet how is it rational? But in the end our author seems to adopt the Promethean attitude he previously condemned:

To man condemned to annihilation, it remains only to cherish the lofty thoughts that ennoble his little day, proudly defiant of the irresistible forces that tolerate for a moment his knowledge and his *condemnation*.

Admiration or condemnation — which? Both together, or in turn? Anything you like, or what suits the humour of the hour? The only condition to keep and preserve your rational freedom is the denial of God, the negation of divine wisdom and divine goodness. It is not to be wondered at, then, that Bertrand Russell found his first essay on "The Freeman's Worship" unsatisfactory and tried another scheme of religion for the use of the rational atheist, "The Essence of Religion," which was published in the *Hibbert Journal*.

THE WORSHIP OF INFINITY

In that second essay Bertrand Russell makes an important admission: that religion is easier with a dogma and the belief in God than without it. But the man of science has no choice. On the one hand, religion is a need; he cannot live without it. On the other hand, belief has become for him an impossibility. He must find some way of inventing a religion without dogma. So the author gives a new definition of what is meant by that need. Religion, for him is:

a certain attitude towards the world, a certain habitual

direction of our thoughts; a life, on the whole, free from the finiteness of self and providing an escape from the tyranny of desire and daily cares.

We have then as an object of our religion: Infinity. Such Infinity exists in ourselves, as an unbounded desire, or negatively, as an impatience at the limits of our self. Infinity longs for infinity.

The infinite part of life does not see the world from one point of view; it shines impartially, like the diffused light on a cloudy sea.

Diffused and confused light! But let us retain another word that is significant: "Impartiality." All the theory can be summed up in a short sentence: Religion is an impartial worship of infinity. That infinity is nothing else than the limitless Universe, and as it is mixed with good and bad, or to speak with more exactitude, as it is neither good nor bad according to our human notions of goodness, our worship needs must be impartial. The impartiality of this religion is an answer to the indifference of its object, though from another passage it would seem that the infinity of the object does not really belong to it, but is rather a projection of the soul's own infinity.

Yet why we should worship and even love Infinity, real or imaginary, we rather fail to see. Is it positive or negative Infinity? Is the Universe to be considered as a real whole, possessing at least the goodness of unity in diversity, an order of parts, or is Infinity a synonym of illimitable confusion? If we keep the initial assumption of the purposelessness and meaninglessness of the Universe, infinity is but an external denomination for an innumerable multitude of objects without any intelligible mutual connexion — an infinity of atoms, with no more interest for man than an infinity of pebbles. Or is it an Infinity of gaseous matter? Or do we contemplate or imagine pure, barren, meaningless infinity? Shall we love and worship Infinity for infinity's sake?

There is indeed an infinity of mercy which is divine. "The

quality of mercy is not strained." But if the walrus and the Carpenter were moved to tears by an infinity of sand, theirs was hardly an attitude of religious reverence. It seems to me that if we want at any price to invest the Whole with august and even lovable infinity, we cannot escape *belief* in some dogma of some soul of goodness in the Whole. Otherwise, is it not a sort of wilful self-deception?

> Mysticism [rational or irrational?] interprets this experience [of infinity?] as a contact with a deeper, truer, more unified world than that of our common beliefs.

The condition of the contact is a complete giving up of all personal will. The vision (objective or subjective, real or imaginary?) of the Infinite, is the reward of absolute disinterestedness.

> The transition from the life of the finite self to the infinite life in the whole, requires a moment of absolute self-surrender when all personal will seems to cease . . . and the soul feels itself in passive submission to the universe.

Submission implies the acknowledgement of some power. Submission, then, to a power beyond us, neither good nor bad but infinite, on account of the infinity! Love of that infinity, wilful abandonment of all humanly intelligible love, hope and desire in order to be able to be totally absorbed in that unintelligible infinity!

What follows is perplexing enough. It must be the description of a mystic state and as such it is not open to discussion. Still, I cannot help inserting here and there some notes of interrogation.

> There arises in the soul [after we have abandoned the pursuit of some strong desire] a state of suspension of the will. . . .

(*Sans amour et sans haine,* says the French poet; without desire or fear. But he adds: *Mon coeur a tant de peine.* It is sad, very sad indeed.)

> when the soul no longer desires or seeks to impose itself

upon the world, but is open to every impression that comes
to it from the world . . .

(Good or bad impression? — then the world has a moral character. Indifferent? then why?)

It is at such a time that the contemplative vision comes
into being, bringing with it universal love and universal
worship. . . .

(Again, is this rational speech? Is it assertion of a discovery in
the world of some beauty, some goodness worthy of our love?
Or is it an unaccountable, gratuitous, but exalting and pleasant self-delusion?)

From universal worship comes joy, from universal love
comes a new desire. . . .

(Hadn't we abandoned all desire? Was it not the condition
of the blissful mystical state?)

. . . and thence the birth [most mysterious!] of that seeking after universal good which constitutes the will of our
infinite nature. . . .

(In accordance with, or in spite of the infinite nature of the
universe?)

Thus from the moment of self-surrender [to absurdity,
purposelessness, inhumanity] which to the finite self [finite,
but wide-awake and logical] appears like death, a new life
begins, with a larger vision, a new happiness and wider
hopes.

(That is an infinite, wilful illusion, a fool's paradise of infinity if, according to the original assumption — which we
must never get weary of repeating, however tedious the repetition — the Whole, the atomic infinity, has no more meaning,
no more goodness, than a single atom, a single pebble.)

But Mr. Russell anticipates our objection. Of course, says
he, such a disposition of mind, such a state of blissful worship
and love and joy and hope is easier to one who believes: "in
an all-wise God, to whom submission is a duty." There are

three elements of Christianity "which it is desirable to preserve if possible": worship, acquiescence, and love.

It is less difficult to acquiesce in what we cannot change,
the indifference of the unresponsive universe in which our lot
is cast, through which our destiny is to acquiesce in our necessary wretchedness and hopelessness. But what of worship
and love? Here, when the case is all but lost, the author finds
occasion to triumph. Worship and love are all the more disinterested and pure in the absence of any worthy object. We
said in the beginning that the essence of Mr. Bertrand Russell's Religion could be expressed in two words: Infinity and
Impartiality. We have discussed Infinity; let us now turn to
Impartiality.

THE RELIGION OF BOUNDLESS UNREASON

Worship may choose its object. There is indeed "a selective
(and simply intelligent and intelligible) worship which demands that its object shall be good," and that worship is not
bad in itself. Only it is of a lower quality. But there is, too,
an "impartial worship, regardless of goodness and badness."
The conclusion, then, is: Let us by all means keep our *selective* worship for a definite and intelligible good. Only that
good is ideal, has no reality. But let us give our *impartial*
worship to the Whole which is not good, for that very reason
that it is not good, namely, that it has no good for us.

Here is *amour pur* with a vengeance! For such worship,
devoid of fear and hope and reverence, worship for the sake
and the beauty of worship, is pure love as well. I do not see
the difference between the two terms.

> The dualism of good and bad, when it is too strongly
> present to our minds, prevents impartial contemplation and
> interferes with universal love and worship.

It is all the difference between earthly and divine love, but
not quite in the Platonic or Spenserian sense:

> Selective, earthly worship which is given to what is de-

lightful, beautiful and good, and the impartial, heavenly love which is given to all indifferently. . . .

To the divine love, the division of the world into good and bad, though it remains true, seems lacking in depth.

Heavenly Love, sublime, groundless, and bottomless!

Moreover, that need of goodness is a residue of dogmatic superstition in the mind imperfectly purified:

In order to free religion from all dependence upon dogma, it is necessary to abstain from any demand that the world shall conform to our standards. Every such demand is an endeavor to impose ourselves upon the world.

Still, we must not give up selective love altogether. It seems the true religious spirit is made of a combination of the two:

The two worships subsist side by side, without any dogma [dogma is the only evil; once free from dogma we may combine the most heterogeneous elements, reason and unreason] . . . the one involving the goodness but not the existence of its object, the other involving the existence but not the goodness of its object. Religious action is a continuous endeavor to bridge the gulf between the objects of these two worships by making more good exist and more existence good.

But then one good is subordinated to the other, the divine to the earthly. Religious worship is with a purpose, and a selfish purpose, that of realising some good, and making the world good at least in part, in spite of itself.

How this consideration agrees with the theory and apology of pure, disinterested love, indifferent to good and evil, I cannot see, but my lack of penetration is due no doubt to dogmatic prejudice, to the confusion of brain induced by dogma; for Mr. Russell, though he recognises the greater effectiveness of Christian belief, thinks that it is due to a "confusion of thought." On the contrary, I should say that Christian belief owes its effectiveness partly to the clearness and distinctness of its premises and to its logical coherence. From the dogma of a good God, Creator of the Whole, and of man, immanent in and transcendent to the conscience of man, there follows rationally enough the belief in the absolute value of the human person, the idea of moral good and of sin, the Commandments, of which the first is to adore God only, to love God and our fellow men for the sake of God. That at least is intelligible.

It is not so easy to see the rationality of Mr. Bertrand Russell's scheme or schemes of rational religion. I omit the discussion of the initial postulate: the meaninglessness and the godlessness of the Universe. I say postulate, for it is not an *a priori* evidence, nor is it a legitimate conclusion of science. Science, modern physical science, excludes from its object the idea of purpose, goodness or beauty, limiting the enquiry to the quantitative aspect of natural things and the relations between phenomena which can be expressed mathematically. It is limitation of the object, not denial of what *is* besides it. And it stands to reason that it cannot conclude anything as to purpose, value, goodness, or beauty. But, granting the postulate, does Russell succeed in giving a rational object to his religion in a Godless Universe? He gives too many objects, and not one of them strikes me as perfectly rational.

The first object may be described as human ideals of goodness, which the good man imagines he can realise. But in these we merely find another irrational assumption — that in spite of the total universal meaninglessness, moral goodness still preserves a meaning. This is impossible and an outrage to reason. Besides, Religion is essentially worship, as Mr. Russell says more than once, and what one worships must be higher and greater than the worshipper. But the reality of human ideals is man himself, his own (absurd and gratuitous) goodness. It is an object of self-congratulation, not of worship.

The inadequateness of that first solution does not escape Russell. He feels that there is in religion a sense of infinity, universality. Let us, then, take as our object the Whole. But again, as the Whole is infinitely meaningless and oppressive of whatever we conceive as beauty and goodness, so the religious attitude will not be worship, but condemnation, defiance, in the name of all that man conceives as good. The Promethean solution!

Russell himself is not slow to perceive the irrationality. Prometheus may well defy Zeus as an unjust tyrant and an evil and malignant power, but the whole is no more evil than it is good; it is simply "things." What does reason say? Submit to the unavoidable, and make the best of it! Call this rational wisdom, but not religion.

Let us try another way out for the difficulties Mr. Russell has created. That hopeless struggle of a rational and moral being in an overpowering infinity, irrational and amoral, is represented as tragic, an awful tragedy, to be contemplated with awe. Between tragic awe and the religious sense, the difference is negligible. Let it be so, but is the spectacle truly tragic? Tragedy is a struggle between hostile forces. But here there is no hostility, unless we choose to deceive ourselves and suppose that the Universe has some hostile intention, an evil *meaning*. Is the self-deception rational?

Let us, then, consider in the Whole nothing more than the character of Infinity. Infinity is beyond us and encompasses us. We may well worship, and even bring ourselves to love Infinity for itself, we are told, irrespective of good or evil; our religion will then be all the loftier, our love all the purer!

Such seems to be the last effort of Mr. Bertrand Russell to provide the freeman with a rational "religion." But as he (very rationally) doubts its effectiveness, he advises us to mix together selective and impartial love and so succeeds in making confusion worse confounded!

That honest and painstaking rationalist philosopher, Emmanuel Kant, conceived a sorry and meagre system of Religion "within the bounds of pure reason." Mr. Bertrand Russell possesses more style, imagination, fire; he is ten times more entertaining, but however pure his rationalistic intent, his genius cannot bear the narrow limits of rationality. His "freeman's worship" may be truly called "the religion of boundless unreason."

CHAPTER FOUR

WELLS' INVISIBLE KING

MR. WELLS IS A WITNESS TO THE RELIGIOUS NEED of the time and the necessity of some sort of religion if one is to be saved from despair. As regards the world at large he is a pessimist; he will not see in it any sign of purpose, at least of a purpose for good. On the contrary, nature seems to be evil. In the sentient world of man and beast everything tends to make life painful. Pain, bodily pain, is the condition, the beginning and the end of life. The stupidity of man, we are told, greatly aggravates this by common religious prejudices and the dogmas of official religions which have made matters much worse. The jungle is bad enough, but it is paradise compared with the hopeless muddle of modern society. In official and dogmatic Christianity, including its ministers, there is no hope of salvation. Clerics of any colour and hue make life more dreary and burdensome.

Still, our time is one of "exceptional religious need," and as there is no religion without some God, it stands to reason that never was a God more sorely needed. Mr. Wells cheerfully comes to us, therefore, with the good news of the one true God, a Gospel which he thinks is not altogether unlike the Gospel of Jesus. Only it excludes the dogma of Creation and God's Fatherhood. It keeps the idea of redemption, but not of redemption through the Redeemer's self-sacrifice and obedience even unto death. It is the Gospel without the Cross; a gospel of war against evil.

84

Its God is not God the Father, nor is he the Son of God. He is our brother, born among men and born of men's wills, but still to any one of us an elder brother, much stronger than we, free from our individual weaknesses, stern of will and inflexible in determination, our leader in the fight. Of such a God Mr. Wells has a revelation and an absolute certitude. He is positive that anybody will have the same if only he "be attentive to the small still voice in his heart."

Before the Wellsian revelation there had been no God for man to put his trust in, no divine leader in the fight against evil. Mr. Wells does not deny that there are powers at work in the Universe. He admits that as a natural philosopher one may and must postulate a cosmic God or a Creator (the name does not matter much). Others may admire and worship in him the Artist or the God of Science. But he has no moral attributes, he remains an absolute stranger to the interests of human life, to man's idea of good and evil, to his struggle for a better life, a more healthy, and socially more just, happy, and peaceful existence. Of all that, the Veiled Being knows nothing, and in its own turn is, and remains, to man "enigmatical and incomprehensible." The best we can do is to ignore it.

Then there is Nature, Life, the streams of Life, the Life-force in which and through which we are and live and move. Life that makes all that is good or bad, beautiful or ugly; the tiger and the lamb, the poisonous snake, the bird, man and woman, beauty and lust, the puzzled and wandering mind, love and hate. Its universal rule is the will to live, the blind struggle for life. Is it good? Is it evil? It is neither. It is not God; it is simply *Life*.

Briefly, there is in the first place the "Unknowable," or the Cosmic God, infinitely remote, inhuman, indifferent, an idle object of speculation. Second, there is nature, living or inanimate, in which man is born but which may be considered apart from man who, as a moral being is, so to speak, an exception and a stranger in nature. Lastly there is man, the

paradoxical creature, a child of nature and a struggling thing
of lust like all the other animals, with a law of his own which
contradicts his lust and sets him above nature. Then there is
God, the God of man, a finite being as we are, born in this
world but concentrating in himself all our desires for a better
world, our fighting disposition, a brother more than a father;
not almighty, but stronger than we are, our leader in the
fight.

God comes, we know not whence, into the conflict of life.
He works in man and through man. He is a spirit, a single
spirit and a single person; he has begun and he will never
end. He is the immortal part, the leader of mankind. He
has motives, he has characteristics, he has an aim. He is, by
our poor scales of measurement, boundless love, boundless
courage and boundless generosity. He is our friend and
brother and the light of the world. That briefly is the belief
of the modern mind with regard to God. There is no very
novel idea about this God, unless it be the idea that he had
a beginning.

Modern religion appeals to no revelation, no authorita-
tive teaching, no mystery. The statement it makes is, it
declares, what we all may perceive and experience.

Our God then, is finite and has a beginning. And his existence is a fact of experience. How then is he born? How and
when does he reveal himself to the mind? A fact of today and
yesterday, like "a beautiful thing we find by the wayside, or
better still the meeting of a friend."

The prelude to the revelation is our inner dissatisfaction
with the world, the distress caused by the view of evil, and
the sense of our helplessness. It is that sense of hopeless confusion which is described as the "conviction of sin." Then
comes as a relief a faint gleam of hope, a glimpse of a divine
force pervading the world of consciences, a universal hope
and will, something like a collective mind. Why not a real
person? We are inclined to welcome the presence as a person,
but we dare not believe and we resist the impulse. But, "in
spite of our resistance, suddenly, in his own time, God comes."
There grows in the mind an "absolute certainty that one is

not alone in oneself." It is not our better self, but a different, brotherly self, "beyond measure wiser, steadfast and pure of aim."

> One is assured that there is a Power that fights with us against confusion, the confusion and evil within us and without. . . .
> There comes into the heart an essential happiness and courage.

What then, is the newly revealed God? And first, what is he not? He is not the God of clergymen and priests. He is not a magician, a miracle worker, altering the course of nature to reward his friends, the just, or to punish his enemies. It is quite useless to pray to him for a favourable change in the weather. With or without a miracle, he does not arrange things for our good. He is not Providence. He is not the vigilant angel, removing obstacles in our way:

> He does not guide our feet. He is no sedulous governess, restraining and correcting the wayward steps of men.

Whatever we undertake to do, we must take our own risks and face the peril.

> But God will be with you nevertheless. In the reeling aeroplane or the dark ice-cave, God will be your courage. He will be with you as you face death; he will die with you as he has died already countless myriads of brave deaths. He will come so close to you that at the last you will not know whether it is you or he who dies, and the present death will be swallowed up in his victory.

That eloquent passage strikes me as more lyrical than real, and rather ambiguous. What does the brave man experience in the hour of his death? The feeling that his God is dying with him, or on the contrary that in his [the brave man's] death, God triumphs and asserts His own victory over death?

Again, God is not the God of the indolent mystic, but of the men of action. God is not the avenger of crime; he does not punish. (And as we shall see, the notion of *sin*, moral evil distinct from ignorance and blunder, and responsibility, in that theology, is rather confused.) And especially he will not punish the so-called sins of impurity. Our God "is not sexual." He has nothing to do with the arbitrary rules theologians have invented in sexual matters. That does not mean that Mr. Wells' own theology advocates anarchy in such matters, but he simply refers them to health, individual and social, and leaves the individual free to determine in his conscience what is harmful and what is right and harmless in sexual relations as in the use of food and drink. And if he is doubtful, let him consult a doctor. In a word, there is nothing specifically sacred in the question of sex.

As to God's positive attributes, first we must bear in mind that he is truly, not metaphorically, a *person*. This means, I suppose, a being, distinct from each of us and from the whole, having a mind and a will of his own. This is "the central article, the axis" of the modern religion:

> God is a person who can be known as one knows a friend, who can be served and who receives service, *who partakes of our nature* . . . [a man then? a greater man? a superman?] who is, like us, in conflict with the unknown and the limitless and the forces of death. He is our King to whom we must be loyal, he is our captain. He feels us and knows us; he is helped and gladdened by us. He hopes and attempts. He is as real as a bayonet thrust or an embrace. . . .

This last sentence is not enlightening. There is indeed something very personal in an embrace, and even in a bayonet thrust. But neither can be said to be a person. How is the Invisible King and God, born in time of distress and hopes, a *distinct* person? How and when does he acquire that personality? Is he now independent of our wills? Does he remain what he is with steadfast will and immovable purpose independently and in spite of what men actually think or feel?

Mr. Wells' answer comes to this: God is a person as the individual man is a person. But what human personality is for the writer remains a mystery, and we cannot expect God's personality to be more clear. What do we mean when we

speak of man as a person? First we imagine a much greater
and more persevering unity than there is in nature.

> We forget that he [this or that man] was once an embryo
> and will presently decay; we forget that he came of two
> people and may beget many. We forget his innumerable
> moods and changes, that he is hardly ever himself. . . .

But what we must not forget, on the other hand, is that he
knows his own changes, that he remembers his past and anticipates the future, that he holds himself responsible for his
past actions! And what still adds solidity to our idea of personality is that people associate personality with the idea of a
body. Without going so far as Christian theology, which tells
us to conceive divine personality as entirely "superior to and
independent of matter," the new religion accepts the conception that a person, a spiritual individual, may be without an
ordinary, mortal body.

> They [the believers in the invisible King] declare that God
> is without any specific body, that he is immaterial, that he
> can effect the material universe — and that means that he
> can only reach our sight, our hearing, our touch — through
> the bodies of those who believe in him and serve him.

Does that mean that he keeps an essential relation to the
bodies of his followers? God, then, would have no individual
body of his own. Neither would he be a pure spirit, but as he
was born of the distress and the nobler feelings which men,
made of spirit and flesh, experience in their soul and in their
flesh, he is still bound up in a mysterious way with the bodily
condition of men. And that brings us to the still more decisive
question: How is the divine person dependent on the conscience of man and the consciences of men?

The answer is, I think, that God is independent of any individual conscience as the human body is independent as
regards this or that particular cell, though it is made of cells.
As man, the human body, is more than a collection of cells,
so this God is other, and more, than a collection of individual

personal wills and thoughts and consciences. He is an original "synthesis." Is he a self-made synthesis? Strange, "passing strange!"

> Modern religion declares that though he [God] does not exist in matter and space, he exists in time just as a current of thought may do; that he *changes* and becomes more, even as a man's purpose gathers itself together; that somewhere in the dawning of mankind he had a beginning, an awakening, and that as mankind grows, he *grows*. . . . With our eyes he looks upon the Universe he invades; with our hands he lays hands upon it. All our truth, all our intentions and achievements he gathers to himself. He is the undying human memory, the increasing human will. [But what is human will in general, and does it increase? How, and in what sense? Mysteries!!]

We must rest satisfied with that explanation and conceive God as a person, whatever be the precise meaning of the term. What then, is this person? What are his moral attributes? He is *Courage*. Wells does not develop the point, but it is clear enough from the whole, that God is mere *strenuousness*. He has all the virtues of the fighter and the leader. What he will become, what will be his occupation and his relations with men when the battle is over and won, is not clear. Will he regulate peace, or even now take interest and pleasure in man's necessary moral holidays? What is certain is that his strenuousness excludes all the attributes of softness and meekness which are to be found in the Gospel. He is not a self-sacrificing God, setting to men the example of self-sacrifice. He is a fighter, and his most appropriate name is *Courage*.

And God *is Youth!* Let us altogether renounce the symbol of God the Father, the Ancient of Days. God began and is always beginning. He looks forever into the future.

> The God of this new age looks, not to our past, but to our future, and if a figure may represent him, it must be the figure of a beautiful youth, already brave and wise, *but hardly come to his strength.* He should stand lightly on his feet in the morning time, eager to go forward. . . .

It is useless to quote the end of the paragraph; it is "litera-

ture," juvenile and sentimental, hardly worthy of Mr. Wells'
mature genius.

That description of the modern God in the whole and in
the details, leaves men with grave misgivings as to his con-
sistency and reality, with doubts about his personality, his relation to the actual conscience of the individual man and of
men; with doubts about his mastery and his leadership, doubts
about his purpose.

> The conception of a young and energetic God, an Invis-
> ible Prince growing in strength and wisdom, who calls men
> and women to his service and who gives salvation from self
> and mortality only through self-abandonment to his service,
> necessarily involves a demand for a complete revision and
> fresh orientation of the life of the convert.

It demands first of all a serious examination as to its reality
and as to his meaning, when he speaks of "the conception of a
spontaneous, developing God arising out of those stresses in
our heart and in the universe, and arising to overcome them."

First, about his spontaneous birth. Is he born "of the
stresses" in each man, first a feeling, a thought, then spon-
taneously a spirit independent of the individual mind, which
remains even when we are no longer experiencing those
stresses? And then is his birth renewed in every heart that
experiences the same distress? Is he the same spontaneous God
with innumerable individual births? It seems that the new
religion imposes on our belief mysteries more startling and
"irrational" than any revelation. One wonders: Did the Invisible King spring up in the mind of our prehistoric ancestor,
the Caveman, one day when he sat puzzling over things, and
finding that "it was a puzzling world indeed" or did he await
the stresses of a more civilised humanity?

If it is said that God is born of many minds, as the body is
one substance, made of many cells, I ask: Were those minds
thinking together? Was it a society of minds united in their
thinking? Then we might conceive the God as that social
spirit which, according to the Durkheim school of sociology,

needs individual consciousness to become manifest, but is independent of individuals and exerts a mastery over them. Only then, there would be as many Gods as there are societies or types of societies. Or again, is he born of the stresses of men living anywhere, dispersed over the world, feeling the same about things in general, unanimous, but without being conscious of this unanimity? How and when will the synthesis be made? Will the God make it? But he is himself "the synthesis!"

What now, about his growth? For he is ever growing — and still ever young — ever learning, through the senses and the brains of men — dependent on the growth of Humanity. But is not mankind getting old, or at least experiencing the lassitude of old age? And if the God depends, in his knowledge and his growth, on the ideas of men and their striving for the betterment of human life, his ideal must change with the generations. Was he the same God, with the same purpose in the Catholic Middle Ages, as he is now in the mind of Wells?

If I were not afraid of being too inquisitive, I would ask Mr. Wells if the God, when he was revealed to his mind, taught him anything new? He is not, we are told, a father, but a brother. Is he an elder or a younger brother? Is he not rather a son of the Philosopher's mind? With Mr. Wells, he hates the waste, the absurdities, and the cruelties of life. But, like Mr. Wells, if his heart is in the right place, his ideas of what is good and what is evil, and of the ideal world which we must fight in order to realise, are less distinct than they are generous.

We have, or at least I have, found great difficulties about the birth and growth of that God, and now we are left uncertain and dubious about the positive good he wants to do, and even about the evil which he is fighting. Mr. Wells does not evade the question. He has a chapter on Sin:

> Let us take up the question of what Sin is, and what we mean by the term "damnation" in the light of this view of human reality.

It is very simple. Without troubling about the origin of the present state of things "we can bring our minds to say that damnation is here; it is the complexus of disharmonies which constitutes our world." Life is a system of disharmonies. It is actual damnation. Hell is the acceptance of the world as it is, a "surrender to limitation; acquiescence in disharmony." Sin? — it is not damnation, but an incidental separation from God. It is more a disease, a case of lunacy than anything else. Is not sin disharmony in man himself, something constitutional which cannot be helped? One would like more light on God's or Mr. Wells' ideas of free will and responsibility.

And when it is said that the world is made of disharmonies, is it the human, social world exclusively, or the world of life at large? I think I remember a passage of Wells on universal suffering, extending his pity to the beasts of the field and the forest, even to the tender feet of the tiger, so easily hurt and pierced by the flints of the thorns, the spikes of the jungle.

What we want is a distinct theory of the supernatural dignity of man, how being born in nature, he can and he must, rise above nature; judge its impulses, their worth, their validity, from some higher point of view; judge even the deepest and most fundamental and, as it seems, necessary impulse, the will to live in the flesh, to persevere in one's temporal being at whatever cost; and how man can decide that in a given case it is better to die than to live.

Life with its disharmonies is damnation. Does the word imply anything more than utter misery in the physical order, damnation for all living creatures, for beast as well as for man? We are born in damnation, Wells informs us, and if we rest satisfied with it, it is hell. It may be mere weakness of mind; it does not seem to imply moral responsibility; it is simply ignorance of the Wellsian God. But once this God reveals himself to the heart of man, once man has made an act of faith, he cannot lose that belief; he is saved. Only it sometimes happens that man accidentally loses touch with this God, and gives in to disharmonies. That is Sin, an incident, an accidental forgetfulness, which does not touch his inmost soul. The assured message is given us that we are still saved in spite of innumerable sins. There is here a kind of Calvinistic comfort. Men seem to be divided into two classes, the damned, namely, those who are lost by nature (but who do not feel their damnation) — and the saved who are confirmed in a state of salvation!

I readily recognise all that is good and generous in Mr. Wells' aspiration towards a better world, though the picture he makes of regenerate humanity in *The Dream* is disappointing. It is almost as dull, as the description of the actual world — its confusion, waste of forces, and hopeless conflict — is in contrast bold and vivid. My contention is that one cannot, logically and convincingly, while remaining on the level of nature, discriminate and judge between the impulses of nature, fight against nature, and set up an ideal above nature. The need of a supernatural belief and of some supernatural God, both immanent and also transcendent to nature, strikes one even more forcibly after reading Wells' *Invisible King* than before. His God may have all the charms of perennial youth, but he has no authority over the mind of men, for truly he is born of man and remains subject to the mind of man. He has no law of his own to impose. A god without a divine right of wisdom, he is *strenuousness,* the symbol of human courage in fighting evil. For Mr. Wells insists on his own (and any individual mind's) liberty of thought even about God. Nay more, God is that Liberty.

> Religion which is free, speaking freely through whom it will, subject to a perpetual unlimited criticism, will be the life and driving power of the whole organized world. [And if you choose to consider the world-state that is to be, as God's church] you may have it so if you will. Provided that you leave conscience and speech and writing and teaching about the Divine things absolutely free, and that you try to set no nets about God. [Such a net would be, I suppose, any definite statement, given as the truth and excluding any conflicting theory!] . . . The World is God's and he takes

it. But he himself remains freedom and we find our freedom in him.

He is our freedom to think and declare anything we like about him? The most debonair of Gods indeed!

The last stroke, the vindication of absolute authority in matters of religion for the individual conscience, seems to me to deprive the Invisible King of the last remnants of godlike prestige. God is liberty, anyone's liberty. What is he for Mr. Wells, except Mr. Wells' actual theory about good and evil?

But he is only the leader of the battle. Of the subject of the fight he has no personal idea and he has to be advised. Each individual follower whispers in the ear of the leader the word of wisdom. Mr. Wells' purpose is self-contradictory. He needs a divine chief to follow and obey, but he is determined that the chief will have no idea or ideal but his own. Finally, in the religious scheme that he proposes, we have a young, ever growing, ever inexperienced, a never mature God, made by man and subject to man's fancy, strenuously waging an endless and hopeless battle against the Almighty power behind the veil, behind and in nature.

That religion is Manicheism, with the faintest and weakest of Ormuzds against an Ahriman of all-crushing power. More exactly, the good God of Wells, the Invisible King, eludes our grasp and vanishes into thin air. But the God whom Mr. Wells in the beginning practically chose to ignore, alone remains according to him most real, the God whom he pictured as the Almighty creator of all the evil in nature, nay of nature which is itself, he holds, thoroughly evil.

The enthusiastic optimism of Mr. Wells is unconvincing. It will strike anyone who has not been privileged with the personal revelation of his God, as a wilful self-deception, the determination to make a Religion of Hope out of a Philosophy of Despair. Logically it ends in religious atheism and we have the assertion of Wells himself that the atheist:

> makes a well meaning gesture in the vacant space. There is no help nor strength in his gesture unless God is there.

Without God, the *Service of Man* [of Sir Harry Johnston, and any similar atheistic core of ethics] is no better than a hobby or a sentimentality or an hypocrisy in the undisciplined prison of mortal life.

We have now come to the conclusion of the negative part of this treatise. It has consisted for the most part in clearing the ground for the actual discussion of the idols with which it was encumbered.

In dealing with Spinoza I have tried to show the powerlessness of rationalism to give us, as an object of religion and as a practical ideal of life, anything more than words; and words, at that, whose only virtue is despair. But a good part of the forces of our adversary has seemed to me to reside in certain nonrational reasons, facts, alleged facts, prejudices, objects of belief — idols, in final analysis, set up by those very men who accuse us of idolatry. The first idol was an assumed Hellenism, represented as an historical ideal of human reason, of art and the wisdom of mankind, which is sovereign and sure of its right to control and absorb the divine. This conception of Hellenism, as we have shown, is but a modern illusion, a recent invention of the imagination, for authentic Hellenism accepts the divine mystery, and far from excluding revelation, admits it to be divine.

There now remains the positive part, for which I should perhaps do better to refer to apologetic treatises. (I may mention here the most recent and one of the most important, the celebrated Conferences of Père Pinard de la Boullaye, at Notre Dame Cathedral.) I can, however, at least offer some confirmations for our faith in the God of Abraham as against the idols of the philosophers, and for the reasons supporting the existence of a divine intervention in our history: human reasons for seeking salvation in a Revelation.

As a transitional chapter, however, we shall first propose our positive moral argument by way of a rejoinder to those who in our day would reject religion altogether, on the score that it has been rendered obsolete by the progress of science.

CHAPTER FIVE

RELIGION AND THE SCIENTIFIC AGE

FOR DECADES OF YEARS, NOW, THE QUESTION HAS been raised periodically whether the findings of science have not outmoded religion. The fact that many of the world's greatest scientists have been Christian believers in the strictest sense of the word sufficiently disposes of that question. It will be well, nevertheless, to devote to it at least a passing consideration.

As a typical illustration we may select an article contributed by Mr. Vanderlaan to *The Journal of Religion* in its issue of April, 1935. It bears the provocative title, "Is Belief Out of Date?" The author's main ideas might be summed up, I think, under the following three points:

1. Whatever may have been said or thought to the contrary, the recent discoveries and theories in physics do not supply the believer with a scientific proof of the existence of God. Consequently unbelief remains the rational attitude of the modern scientific man in the question of God.

2. The question of a cosmological God, a prime mover, or supreme architect and engineer of the material world, without any interest in man's well-being or in his moral life, is purely academic.

3. A belief in a "moral" God as a ground of human morals is useless and futile, since man finds in humanism, or the study of human nature as a fact of experience, both the rule and the means of moral conduct.

Implied in Mr. Vanderlaan's article is the conclusion that belief is now out of date, and has been so ever since the beginning of the modern scientific age. My intention here is to show, quite to the contrary, that belief in God is not and never can be out of date to the moral man; in other words, that some explicit or implicit assertion of a transcendent or supernatural value and reality is necessary as a rational ground of man's moral life. And by supernatural I mean what is above the natural experimental science of man. To the scientist's dogma of the self-sufficiency of man, theoretical and moral, in everything that pertains to rational activity, I oppose the natural need in man of something above nature. I hold, as Father H. Steuart puts it,[1] that

> considered by himself as a being who should be able, without involving any other being, to give a fully satisfying account of himself, man is a failure. . . . Man, studied by the methods which prove so successful when applied to the rest of creation, stubbornly refuses to be explained. He comes under many categories, but under none of them completely; he partakes of many natures but transcends them all.

Before proceeding farther I must explain in a few words the believer's attitude with regard to science: its meaning, its scope, its progress, and its recent discoveries, in relation to his beliefs. That attitude, I am sorry to say, is altogether misrepresented by Mr. Vanderlaan when he suggests that the theist finds in certain scientific theories a decisive argument for the existence of God, and even that there is no other proof; and that the certitude that God exists is bound up with Eddington's interpretation of the most recent data of physics.

The alleged positive argument thus established could be put in this form: Where science fails to explain the facts of nature, supernatural will and power are required as a cause. But we have of late found in the first elements of matter and their mo-

---

[1] Steuart, *The Inward Vision* (London: Longmans, Green & Co., 1931), p. 45.

tion an indetermination and a spontaneity such that science is unable to foresee and explain what may or may not happen in the future. Therefore it is necessary to postulate a super-natural will and power which we call God. But, says Mr. Van-derlaan, exposing the weakness of the supposed argument: "Ignorance cannot be the open door to certitude. If science cannot tell us as well as once it claimed, what reality is, that is more reason, not less, for agnosticism. A time when science is in difficulties is precisely not the time to say it has discovered God."

To that I answer, and I am sure that any theist who knows the grounds of his belief would answer the same: First, the reasons for belief in God are independent of science, positive or experimental, with its postulates and self-appointed limits, since they are of a different and superior order. Science has for its object observable facts and their laws, or relations of nec-essary sequence or simultaneity. That there is between phenomena such a necessary sequence is not an *a priori* evidence, nor can it be scientifically demonstrated. It is a postulate which can be interpreted in many different senses. And it is a fact that when men of science care to investigate the grounds and value of their principles, the greatest diversity prevails among them.

We must bear in mind the essential difference between *science* which has for its object the laws of phenomena but remains abstract and hypothetical as to the existence of things, and *philosophy* which starts from the fact of existence as such, and seeks the causes of that existence. Not only, then, does the theist not conclude the existence of God from any scientific fact or theory, but he is sure that scientific investigation and reasoning, if it be careful not to transgress its own rules, can-not possibly interfere with his own conclusions.

Second, I answer that it often happens that certain scien-tists, and unbelievers of the "scientist" type, do transgress those rules and make their negation of God dependent on scientific determinism, taken as an absolute and necessary law of things. For them the sequence of events of any observable order is ruled by the same necessity as mathematics; and as mathematics excludes all consideration of efficiency and finality, so does the knowledge of nature. Consequently, if it happens that the very progress of scientific investigation throws some doubt on the absolute character of determinism in physics, and points to indetermination and spontaneity in the inmost heart of nature, the dogmatic unbeliever and scientist will have some reason to be genuinely distressed. The believer, on the other hand, will have some reason to rejoice, not for himself but for the sake of the unbeliever; not that science has proved the existence of God, for it can neither prove nor disprove it, but because science itself has removed a prejudice which was for some of its devotees an obstacle to the rational belief in the existence of God.

Let me now discuss the main point at issue: the necessity to the moral man of the belief in God. Kant speaks of two facts of inexhaustible wonder: the starry heavens above our heads and the moral law in our souls. Each testifies to the divine. But I pass over the starry heavens and the order of the physical universe to consider only the fact of moral consciousness. Indeed, I am convinced that there is a valid cosmological argument for the existence of God, but I am ready to concede to Mr. Vanderlaan that, if from nature, outside man, we could infer only a cosmological God, as Aristotle, for instance, seems to do — a God without a relation to man's moral life — such a question of God would be merely academic. But I maintain, moreover, that man finds in his very conscience the evidence of a God, of the soul, etc. That this God of man's moral world is the God of the material universe can, I think, just as truly be demonstrated. But it is a different question altogether, one into which I need not enter now.

Therefore, I argue that man's, any man's, moral life, his idea of duty, of a good transcending any kind of private gratification, of a supreme and an absolute good, the only good which makes life worth living — in a word, everything which makes up the moral life of man — is all bound up with the explicit or implicit belief in a God — a moral, personal God, a God who is our living law, our living Providence and love: the perfect expression of such divine reality which is none other than the Christian dogma of the divine fatherhood.

Against such a view Mr. Vanderlaan holds what we may call the dogma of the moral self-sufficiency of man. He writes in the beginning of his article (p. 222): "It ought by now to be clear that idealistic strivings contain their own rewards, and that valid moral imperatives correspond to basic desires of human nature." Now what I do not find perfectly clear in that sentence is how Mr. Vanderlaan makes any distinction between the fact of basic desires and the idea and validity of a moral imperative; whether the idea of duty has for him any value beside the fact of our instinctive strivings; whether our basic desires or instinctive strivings are truly idealistic, and what the scientific meaning of ideal and idealistic really is; and, finally, what those moral imperatives which correspond to our basic desires are.

We have a partial and only a partial answer to these questions where Mr. Vanderlaan writes:

These moral imperatives which spring from innate impulses, like the love of justice and the hate of suffering, need no superhuman support, nor could they be more commanding if uttered by a voice from Sinai. It is needless to inquire why we ought to care about our neighbor or about future generations. The fact is that normal humanity has those interests. If altruism formed no part of our natural constitution, it could be no more binding on us than it is on stones. But the fact that sheer brute selfishness does not satisfy our full body of desires forms an adequate basis for morality, regardless of academic questions about the universe.

There is still, to my mind, some obscurity there. But I take it to mean that altruism or unselfish devotion to other people's good, or to a common good, has become a part of man's nature; that the question of duty or of moral imperative, of an "ought," beside the fact of instinct, is not merely academic but altogether idle and meaningless, as it is idle to inquire why we should eat or sleep, since normal humanity eats when it is hungry and goes to sleep when it is tired. Just as the man made out of brute humanity by Dr. Moreau in Wells' tale had to repeat to himself the command to walk on two legs. But whatever may be thought, said, or guessed about our animal ancestry, it is a fact that the actual human biped, the normal biped, walks on two legs, and has not the least sense of a duty of doing so. Fact is, indeed, stronger than duty!

Therefore Mr. Vanderlaan acknowledges an actual opposition between instinct, some natural instincts, and the moral imperative or the instinct of altruism. Consequently, he is bound to give some reason why normal humanity should follow one instinct rather than another. At any rate, he cannot dismiss the question as idle and academic. Moreover, there is a certain lack of precision, a vagueness in the definition of those moral imperatives, which have become natural impulses as justice and the hate of suffering, which our author puts side by side. Justice and the hate of suffering — that is rather perplexing for me. The hate of suffering, as such, is very human, but it does not strike me as bearing an essential relation to justice or to altruism. It seems to me that it is, on the contrary, strongly individualistic if not selfish. It begins at home, and too often it ends at home. Now, the idea that suffering, and especially bodily suffering, is such an absolute evil that it must be avoided at any price — that I consider as simply immoral.

Pain, Socrates would say, is foreign to good or evil, irrelevant to virtue. Pain may be good, and pleasure, especially sensual pleasure, may be bad. It is certainly bad, and is the source of all injustice if pursued as an end for its own sake. Pain is given us with pleasure to make virtue out of it. Indifference to pain is a condition of moral virtue. I should say more: That pain is, in the actual state of man, the condition of moral progress; it has a purifying and strengthening effect which, if borne bravely, makes the human heart stronger and more compassionate as well. As Coventry Patmore has so excellently put it:

> O Pain, love's mystery,
> Close next of kin,
> To Joy and heart's delight,
> Low pleasure's opposite,
> Choice food of sanctity
> And medicine of sin. . . .

Whatever certain scientists may think, such a sense of the value of pain is a fact in certain souls, and these the most noble souls. What a pity it would be, indeed, if ever it should become out of date!

But that is, after all, only a secondary point. And I suppose the fault is rather in the expression than in the actual thought itself. Consequently, I shall confine myself to what is, no doubt, the essential part of morality, or of moral instinct, according to Mr. Vanderlaan: care about our neighbor or about future generations, or, as we say in common parlance — altruism.

Is such altruism a dominant fact, an instinct normally prevailing over other contrary instincts? Is the modern man more altruistic than selfish? Or if instinct is not yet strong enough, does positive science supply what is wanting, and afford a clear and effective rule of social good conduct? It may be so in some secret paradise, at Los Gatos, or in the immediate neighborhood, perhaps; but what strikes the observer is the rather alarming progress of individualism, the questioning of altruistic principles, which in a less enlightened age were not, at least as rules of conduct, open to discussion, but were admitted unreservedly.

I will not deny that there is an instinct of altruism or self-devotion. There has always been. A thoroughly selfish, self-centered individual could not live. A certain generosity has always been a law of life. But the individualistic instinct is, to say the least, as strong — the will to live, to persevere in one's being by whatever means nature puts at our disposal. But shall we say that such an instinct to live has been superseded by altruism? I doubt it, as I see no evident signs of it; but, on the contrary, an alarming revival of rationalistic individualism. The devotion of self to any common cause, to any social group, has never been so freely open to discussion and doubt as at the present time. All social and national bonds seem to be relaxed and the individual left to himself to find his own individual happiness, and to use to that effect the resources of modern civilisation. What still binds nations or social groups together is rather a community of fear and hate, not a common ideal of good, not a spontaneous mutual love.

Certainly the instinct to reason out principles and dogmas and impulses has never been stronger than now in this enlightened twentieth century. Man is, indeed, a rational animal, and reason has the power to weaken irrational instincts. And once we begin to reason out our altruistic instinct, a multitude of questions arises on the meaning of altruism itself. We have all heard that man must love his neighbor as himself. But what does love of my neighbor mean? The precept has a clear sense in Christian theology and practice; not so in a strictly scientific society, and from the point of view of positive science. And who is my neighbour? What individual or group or common ideal has a claim to my love? Does the parable of the good Samaritan express an instinct of the modern man? Outside of Christianity I do not see that there is a unanimous answer to the momentary question: What is that man, that human nature, whose perfection and whose welfare I have perpetually — and shall I say instinctively? — at heart, even though it be against my individual interests? What is "man" for the modern man? Merely a name conveniently applied to beings who are more or less like myself in bodily structure and the faculty of speech. But is mere likeness sufficient to stir in me an instinct of special consideration, respect, and benevolence? Has the most modern man the same consideration for all men alike, whatever be their race or their colour? Is the Negro, for instance, always and everywhere a "neighbour," a brother to the white man? What is the value of a brown-skinned anthropoid, gifted with articulated speech, compared to the value of a good horse or of my old faithful dog? I may need a faith, a strong faith — I do not mean to make a difference between the two but to decide in favour of the grinning anthropoid. It is not a question of what we feel to be a duty, though opposed to impulse, but rather of the instinctive impulse which it is my duty to resist and conquer. But, omitting the doubts arising from the difference of race or colour, there is the question among civilised men of the qualities one must fulfil to be entitled to the respect of other men, to be accounted a man with the full rights of humanity, or even with any right at all. What, for instance, must be the attitude of men (of the state or of the individual) toward the helpless, the apparent cases of humanity, which, through disease, are altogether inefficient, useless, a mere burden to society, even a danger, for disease, any disease, is in some degree contagious? Is it healthy for man to devote his life to the service of such degraded humanity, of the lepers, for instance? Is it rational and scientific to follow such an impulse of pity for the poor and the helpless? In a word, is there still outside Christianity a living idea, an instinct, of the dignity of man as man?

There is still another question which does not appear to be solved either by instinct or by scientific reason: which of the two forms of altruism, the love of the living, individual man, or the love of humanity in the abstract, are we to practice? or how reconcile them? Have future generations, men as yet unborn, the same right to our care, nay more, even a greater right, than the actually living man who is soon to die? There have been, and there are still even now, fanatics all the more dangerous for the sincerity of their altruism, in whom the idolatry, the worship, of some abstract, ideal superman has destroyed all regard for the well-being of their immediate, actually living and suffering neighbour. The priest, or the Levite, who looked on the poor man lying wounded by the wayside and passed on, may have been such an idealist. Each instinct if not exclusive is right: love of mankind and the progress of mankind and of future generations, love of my fellow traveler in the present ways of life, even self-love are all right. And self-love is good, fundamental, and necessary. But the harmonious and living synthesis of these impulses is not effected by mere development of instinctive value or by any scientific reason. Rather, I maintain that it needs a higher and a divine principle: a real unity binding the individual with the whole, not absorbing and losing it in the whole.

Let us look at the problem more closely. Kant's formula of duty was good but incomplete: "Always treat humanity, both in your person and in the persons of others, as an end and never merely as a means." But the real spring of morality is respect and love, not alone respect, but respect joined with love; love and respect not of an abstract principle such as "law," but of something real which makes any man worthy, both of reverence and of love, such as I should not hesitate in certain cases to sacrifice my pleasure and interest to his well-being, even to risk my life for his.

But what makes a man, any man, an object of reverence to another man must be something superior to mere human nature, a more than human value. That more than human value I call divine. It must be an essential relation to a reality which claims absolute reverence or adoration. In other words I revere God in man, and any man ought to revere God in his poor human self, however naturally faulty and defective.

But, again, mere reverence without love will achieve nothing. Self-devotion requires love; I must love my neighbour as myself. But why? Because that essential relation to God in man is one of sonship. God is the father of all men. That divine fatherly love of all and each is the principle of a divine equality between men: a veritable bond of brotherly love. Consequently, it might be shown that such dogma of divine fatherhood or a more or less distinct anticipation of that dogma is at the basic origin of religion, the very essence of religion; and that it is at the same time the bond of human society and the principle of individual freedom.[2] It cannot be scientifically proved or disproved, and it does not run the risk of becoming obsolete, so long as the conflict in the human soul between self-love and altruism, between the devotion to human society and the love of and devotion to the individual human person, has been solved by science or philosophy.

In a word, if belief is out of date, morality is out of date as well; and we see no sign of instinctive agreement between men on these essential points of morality — now less than ever before. I can only suggest here that the consideration of the meaning of human life from the point of view of death would bring us to the same conclusion on the subject of belief.

We may agree with Spinoza that philosophy, the philosophy implied in any rational life, ought to be a meditation not on death but on life. But still the fact of death cannot be overlooked. On the contrary, if we are in earnest, if we do not want to deceive ourselves, we must look the hateful fact in the face, and our meditation ought to be of life in death and through death — how death can be conquered and how immortality secured. It might be shown that there is no instinct which makes the idea of death, as the absolute end beyond which there is no hope of survival, tolerable to the modern man; that such meditation is beyond the scope of experimental science, is rather of the supernatural order; and that, consequently, the belief in the personal and living God as the guaranty of our own life beyond death is not and never shall be out of date.

———

[2] Cf. Hocking, *The Meaning of God in Human Experience.*

CHAPTER SIX

GOD AND HISTORY

FICHTE LAYS DOWN AS A NECESSARY CONDITION
of moral action the affirmation of the reality and value of the
world, to which we cannot conclude by means of discursive
reason alone. This secure assertion he would call *faith,* and
though he opposes it to a sterile and despairing rationalism, it
is really a guarantee of reason. For the use of reason is founded
on principles which reason cannot demonstrate, and the necessary trust we put in these principles may well be called
faith.

Brunschvicg is pained at this romantic deviation from the
straight path of reason. Whether it was due to infidelity to
rationalism, or to a distraction or weakness, or just a mistake,
Brunschvicg prefers to forget it out of respect for the memory
of the great man. In any case, he claims, this lapse has nothing
to do with the progress of conscience.

We claim exactly the opposite. Fichte gave promise of
liberating us from the slavery of rationalism. He showed the
right way; but he failed to follow that right way to its end.
An unfortunate rationalist scruple makes him lose all the
benefit of his salutary course. Like Kant, he wants to keep
religion "within the strict limits of reason." He wants to be a
Christian, but only on the condition of rationalising the history of Christ, of retaining the symbol and rejecting the history
proper. "For history doesn't save; only metaphysics can save."

A fatal sentence that and one that excludes history and re-establishes rationalism, the usurper, on the divine throne. I say "rationalism" and not "reason" because this exclusion of history cannot be made in the name of reason. For reason, conscious of its limits, having had to make an act of faith in its own power, cannot reasonably refuse to be enlightened by "historic" revelation, but rather must be rationally ready to welcome it. Faith, natural or supernatural, is not antirational, but on the contrary answers the expectation of reason itself.

But Fichte will have none of the God of Abraham. Like Brunschvicg, he holds to the God of the philosophers and nothing more. And in so doing he sides with Brunschvicg against himself. Why call upon us to believe, if reason is to remain the absolute mistress, controlling all, explaining all, leaving to the Living God no initiative, forbidding His Providence to manifest itself and His creative goodness to appear at a certain time, in a certain place, to certain men chosen to be His witnesses before all mankind? Would such a manifestation be contrary to reason? "No," we are told, it is not irrational; it is just not rational. "It asks us to submit our minds to the testimony of another, to accept an historic message, the idea of salvation by a man whom God has sent and who is invested with His power, a Saviour, a Redeemer whom men could see and touch. That is beyond the realm of metaphysics. And as such we consider it null and void." And that is as much as to say that there is no God but Metaphysical Reason, a reason that is here understood as not being beyond the reach of a learned man or metaphysician, an Immanent Reason.

The God of Abraham or the God of the scientists. Again we are left with the necessity of making a choice. To be sure, in choosing the God of Abraham, belief transcends reason; but that belief is itself reasonable. At the very least, there is no reason which would forbid reason being transcended by belief in an authentic message. The supreme effort of which reason is capable is the recognition of the existence of God, the all-powerful Creator, and of the divine creative liberty. But this divine liberty has its secret which the human reason clearly cannot penetrate. What is the meaning of this world which is "being made," of this history? Through it must run a divine plan and it must be directed towards divine ends. But in order that we, the actors, and free actors, in this history may worthily collaborate in it, we must have some knowledge of these ends. And this knowledge can be acquired only by a free revelation on the part of God. Our reason does not demand or prove the necessity of a revelation, but it most certainly does not exclude it and men of good will have every motive to expect it.

Shall we say that, though God freely created the world, he has no interest in its history and simply leaves it to evolve and be fashioned haphazardly as human passions direct? The reason that would safeguard the divine impassibility, would free God from this anxiety. But if it follows its respect to its logical conclusions, this reason will have to exclude the divine from all human interest too, individual as well as social. And that would be a return, or retrogradation, to the God of Spinoza, indifferent to all "good."

If there is a Providence of God over man, there is also a Providence of God over human history. The message of God to the man Abraham, the election of a people to be His witness before the nations, the manifestation in Christ, the Word of God made flesh, all that is beyond scientific reason, but is entirely plausible for a higher reason and entirely congruous with the intelligence, the knowledge, we have of the Divine. The risk of faith in the God of Abraham is, if not the most rational, assuredly the wisest of risks. I speak of a "risk" because there is a certain uneasiness which remains even after all the "reasons for believing" have been accepted; for it is faith after all, and our reason, ever unsatisfied — a reason that wants to *see,* restlessly seeking for certitude in its darkness — continues to reason, in order to see. *Pergere cogitare,* to continue to think, is according to St. Thomas the mark of the certitude of faith, human or divine.

Rationalism (not a reason that is modest and conscious of its limits) resists endlessly and gives way only step by step. If it concedes that God may possibly have an interest in His Creation, it limits that interest as far as possible. There is a Providence; granted. But it is a "general" Providence careful to safeguard the admirable general laws wherein its Wisdom is manifested; it is a Providence of salvation for individual souls, but exerting its influence as far as possible within the exact bounds of the laws of nature, with a strict economy of extraordinary manifestations; so much so that any talk of a miraculous intervention should be held suspect *a priori.*

This tribute to His guiding Wisdom wrongs God by the paltry limits which it attempts to set to the liberty of His Creative Love. Being the Creator of the universe and the Creator of human wills, the most humble of which has more worth than all the constellations — human wills born in history, whose exercise is conditioned by history, and who are the workers of history — will not His solicitude be present at every moment of history? And if He is so intimately and lovingly present, shall we dispute His right to appear? In the name of what reason?

We do not say that there is a real necessity or compulsion forcing Him to manifest Himself. His manifestation remains a gift, a favour to humanity, but a favour, a grace most welcome to the mind of man, and one which reason itself, by its impotence to satisfy itself, leads us to anticipate and desire.

And so we hold that if God is personal and a Creator; if He is Providence, Love, Justice; if He is the Creator of history, and if therefore history has a divine meaning, that reason is presumptuous and foolish which would forbid God to manifest Himself historically. Not only is it exceeding its rights, but it is usurping the role of the divinity in pretending to satisfy by itself alone the soul's need for God; and it fails miserably in its undertaking.

The subject of this chapter, then, is "God in History," and man's salvation in and by history, because God, who is infinitely beyond all history, is immanent in history, of which He is the Creator and the creative life. He is the Creator and He calls us to be collaborators in the work of the divinisation of history. Even prescinding from a visible manifestation of God in the world, our reasons for living and dying, our salvation, would be found in and by means of our social and historical activity. It would consist in making ourselves divine by collaborating in the work of divinisation, the work of the realisation of God in history. Only, we would be left to our own rational conjectures to determine the direction and progress this divine work should take. A living revelation whose life is never weakened, a secret but at the same time certain life of God in our history, fulfils the expectation of the human soul and establishes us in the security of religion, of the unique and universal religion.

In this, as in the preceding chapters, it will be of interest to center our remarks in certain individual writers. Many of the points dealt with here we can find expressed in two very valuable works, the first and most recent of which is the collection of *Gifford Lectures* of Mr. A. E. Taylor, published in two volumes under the title *The Faith of a Moralist*.[1] The second is that of the American Philosopher Hocking, whom I have already quoted in the introduction. My allusion here is to his book *The Meaning of God in Human Experience*,[2] which shall be referred to more specifically in the following chapter.

Taylor, starting from the moral fact, deduces its rational postulates. Hocking, beginning with primitive religion, establishes its meaning and from it draws conclusions as to what should be and what *is* religion in its purity and plenitude.

In the first place let us ask: What are the dogmas implicitly affirmed in the idea of the moral act? That is the question

---

[1] The Macmillan Co.
[2] Yale University Press.

proposed by Mr. Taylor. We might put it in another way: What are the postulates of practical reason? And here we prescind entirely from the question of the relation of the practical to the speculative reason as it is presented by Kant.

The conclusions arrived at in the more philosophical part of the work assert the absolute and independent character of duty and obligation . . . and consequently the fact of transcendence. Moral sense is not a blind instinct, but implies a will stronger than any other will, a will that transcends us and imposes itself on our conscience. The moral law is a divine commandment, not of a reason which decides to set itself up as the universal and sovereign lawgiver, but a commandment of God, who is infinitely above us, the Sovereign, so independent of the limits of our conscience that He is intimate to our conscience.

It is not enough to affirm a transcendence. For rationalism will bend all its efforts to immobilise that transcendence and to disengage it from any interest in things temporal. To satisfy rationalism this transcendence must not be human, and must be indifferent to human conduct.

And here Mr. Taylor affirms and proves, in a very beautiful chapter, what he calls the "Initiative of the Eternal." The initiative of an eternal thought, and so a meaning of life which for humanity and the individual alike, transcends the present limits. There must be an eternal interest in human life and an eternal life.

> The whole-hearted acceptance of the postulates of the moral life itself involves an outlook on the world and on man's place in it which is more than merely moralistic. The good man who thinks out to the end the implications of his loyalty to the moral good will find that he is pledged to something more than simple recognition of an ideal of conduct as entitled to his unqualified respect. He is committed to a belief in the final coincidence of the "ought" and the "is" in virtue, of their common source in a transcendent living and personal Good — one, complete, eternal — the only belief which rightfully deserves to be called belief in God. He is also committed to the recognition that

whatever is, other than God Himself, is a creature of God, having the token of its creatureliness stamped upon it by its temporality and "passage"; that for a reasonable creature, such as man, the fundamental concern of life is a reorganization of personality, only possible as a response to an initial movement manwards on the part of the Eternal itself, by which reorganization the creature comes to seek and find its own intimate felicity not in the temporal, but in the abiding; that the very imperativeness of this quest makes it only reasonable to anticipate ultimate attainment in a life no longer condemned to failure, by its inherent successiveness. In a word, we tried to show (in the preceding volume) that the moral life of man, rightly studied, bears impressive testimony to three great strictly *supernatural* or *other-world* realities — God, grace, eternal life.[3]

It seems to me (and I do not think I am departing very much from the thought of Mr. Taylor here) that in the moral fact and even in sin itself, in the consciousness we have of sin, wherein the divine character of obligation is most clearly evidenced, we find proof of the eminent dignity of human nature, of the absolute value of the human soul, of every human soul, through its intimate relation with a personal God, who is the Creator. If, moreover, the soul and human life have a divine and eternal value, then man's surroundings and the conditions of his life participate in that value. There is a divine interest, and therefore a divine value in things, and a divine value of time and of that which is being made in time. In other words, history should be a realisation of the divine and of divine ends. God the Creator of man, of man's time and of his history, exercises over man, over every man, and over time (the whole march of it as well as each moment) and over history, an attentive Providence. Nothing happens that His grace does not foresee. Nothing is made that He does not sustain. And finally, it seems to me, as Mr. Taylor suggests in his first and develops in his second volume, that the hypothesis of a revelation of God in history, of a historical revealed religion, is not contrary to reason, but quite plaus-

---

[3] *Faith of a Moralist*, Vol. II, pp. 1, 2 (The Macmillan Co.).

ible and answers an innate desire. In fact this hypothesis alone can satisfy the moral needs of humanity; that the God of Abraham and the God of Christ is more "efficacious" than the God of the philosophers; that He alone is "efficacious" and that we owe all to His gratuitous revelation.

MORAL CONSCIENCE, SIN AND LAW

The moral imperative and the idea of the absolute good or evil of our conduct is revealed to us in the consciousness we have of our sin. "Whether Adam ever fell or not," says Mr. Taylor, "*I* am a 'fallen creature' and I know it."

That is what we mean by the "sense of sin," the sense of an imputable fall and one for which my will, unaided, is incapable of making reparation. Irreparable if I insist on remaining alone, unforgettable in that case, because my sin is ever before me; or if I forget it, my lot is even worse, for it remains, like a stain, like a shameful mark, like the scar of a whip on the back of a slave. The simile is borrowed from Socrates in Plato's *Gorgias*. The two following paragraphs are only a summary of his doctrine.

Sin, says Socrates, is an evil which, if we took full consciousness of it, would make us actually desire to suffer punishment to expiate it. For all other evils, sickness, sadness, and even death, are wrongly called evils. They may be good for all we know. But sin is an absolute evil.

To commit grievous sin is to ruin one's life in that same instant, in proportion as the sin was voluntary, and to compromise eternity. "It is far better to suffer injustice than to commit it." Evil received is not an evil. It passes and leaves no traces in the soul; but injustice committed, remains.

Plato, in his old age, repeated this message of his master:

> We must firmly believe in these ancient and sacred traditions which reveal to us the immortality of the soul, the existence of judgments and terrible punishments to be undergone when the soul shall be separated from the body.

And that is why we regard it as a lesser evil to be the victims of great crimes or great injustice, than to commit them. The man who aspires to riches and whose soul is narrow and mean, will not listen to this kind of talk. Or if he does, he thinks it a laughing-matter and shamelessly reaches about on all sides to grasp anything he can eat or drink, anything that is capable of procuring for him the satisfaction of that unworthy and gross pleasure which is wrongly called love. That man is blind who cannot distinguish which of his actions must be condemned as impious, and the evil that is always bound up with each of these crimes; and this impiety the unjust soul must necessarily carry with it both in this life and also in the after-life, in all its shameful and wretched peregrinations in the world of shades. (*Letter VII,* 335.)

Of course, one might deny this absolute character of sin, but in so doing, he would do away with all ethics. For certain modern moralists, for instance, sin is nothing but a fact like any other, albeit a regrettable fact. It passes and, though unatoned, nothing remains of it, save perhaps certain temporal consequences which can easily be rectified. But once the sin is committed, to worry ourselves about it would be not only foolish, but wrong. We must simply not think about it any longer; carry on with the game. Our error can be made up for by a better and happier shot later on in the game. To keep our sin ever before our eyes, to feel remorse over it, to *believe* in it, would in the mind of such writers be sin itself — if indeed that word can have any meaning. Meditation on sin is for them a meditation on death. The wise man meditates on life, not on death. And that brings us back to Spinoza, who would forbid us repentance as a weakness.

Sin might also be interpreted scientifically, in the manner of the biologist or sociologist. Then it would be an "abnormal case," a case of "regression." The sinner is a barbarian. He does not enter into the framework of society. Or better still, according to others, sin is normal; normal like the law which prohibits it and like the rod, literally or figuratively speaking, by which it is punished. Law, sin, and rod are all necessary, and all help towards the good of society. But infractions of the law, they argue, are also necessary. If laws were not broken we should have cause for alarm; it would be a sign that the body of society was headed for a fall. Just as in a school, though it is necessary that there be rules forbidding pranks and punishment as an effective sanction of these laws, still it is also necessary for the health of the school that there be pranks. We must not attach a tragic mythology to natural facts. It is superstition that makes us conjure up these imaginings of stains, irreparable marks, and judgement.

Mr. Taylor affirms that it is just the opposite and that the sense of sin is not a contamination of ethics by theological theory, but on the contrary a really moral experience which calls for theological explanation.

But what if I refuse to be bound by this absolute Good and Evil? Why should I not enjoy that "liberty" of which certain psychologists speak as of a conquest of the modern conscience? In that case, I fail to see how you can attribute any meaning or any value to human conduct.

A certain Miss Hawkins, writing at the beginning of the nineteenth century, gives us an idea of what such a "liberated" conscience as opposed to the enslaved conscience of believers, can and should be. Speaking of Samuel Johnson, who as a sincere Christian had the misfortune of taking the Christian law seriously, Miss Hawkins asks indulgence for him:

> Much has been written regarding Johnson's excessive, nay superstitious scrupulousness in religious matters, but in my opinion without considering his natural infirmities.

He beat his breast in repentance for his sins; therefore the poor man must have been suffering from some serious illness!

> Had he realized that the service of the Gospel is perfect freedom, he would have abandoned efforts at self-perfection and lived at ease.

Oh, the wonderful liberty of the Gospel according, not to St. Paul, but to Miss Hawkins!

Arnold Lunn cites this text in his book *Now I See,* and he

adds also one taken from John Hawkins on the same Johnson (Who is this John? No doubt a brother or cousin of
Miss Hawkins. They are certainly kindred souls):

> He had a natural imbecility about him, arising from
> humanity and pity for the sufferings of his fellow-creatures,
> which was prejudicial to his interests.

What wonderful progress, from the Christianity of Johnson
to this perfect balance of moral health in the Hawkinses!
Perhaps other exponents of this wisdom, liberated from the
superstition of an absolute law, would express it less crudely.
But in every case, moral good and evil remain a matter of
taste, of habit or convention.

We have said, then, that in the sense of sin the absolute
character of morality is almost clearly shown. It is from this
as a starting point that we must begin to define the religion
which it supposes or for which it prepares.

There is, in the consciousness of sin, a sense of constraint.
But that constraint does not come, as one might think, from a
will foreign to our own. The constraint is intimate and personal; it is that of the passion which prevents us from effec-
tively wishing, in such or such a case, what we do profoundly
wish and what we cannot help wishing. As Socrates admirably
expresses it: "The sinner does not do what he wishes to do."
Sin sets man's spirit in contradiction with itself. He acts
against his own will. He does just the contrary of what he
really wishes to do, of what he cannot help wishing. But this
will against which he acts in sinning and which is absolute,
cannot come entirely from himself. In that will — which everything within me, all my passions, all that is temporal and
transitory repudiates — we must recognise another, but fully
as intimate an authority. It is a constraining authority, and at
the same time the most intimate of friendships, if we take
friendship to consist, as in fact it does, above all else in a
community of will. Where I am most myself, I am at one with
God, my will makes but one with the will of God. Sin is the

violation, the flouting of this "friendship." It is the refusal
and denial of divine friendship. And it is precisely this that
constitutes the pangs of remorse, the fact that we have outraged divine friendship, the love and majesty of the Infinite
God. Nor is it gross anthropomorphism to speak thus of the
divine "friendship." We cannot speak of God otherwise than
in human, analogous terms. But it often happens, and it is the
case here, that the divine clarifies our ideas of the human. It
is immediately obvious how infinitely the friendship of God
exceeds all that we understand by human friendship. But even
human friendship is a mystery for us. We feel poignantly our
inability to realise towards another man the plenitude of what
we understand by friendship, that full and complete unanimity, as well as the religious respect which it requires, and
without which it never can go beyond the limits of
comradeship.

It is in sins against one's parents that this sense of sin is
most keenly felt, sins of rebellion against them and contempt of
their love, which are deeply felt. A more superficial psychology
would attribute the idea of duty, insofar as it is exterior and
restraining, to the fear of parental authority. But the feeling
of guilt after a sin of disobedience against one's father is due
much more to love than to fear. And the remorse is, in fact,
all the more painful when no punishment follows. For then
the child feels that the fault has been too great, too serious
even to be punished. And the same is true for an act of disobedience of which the father never learns. That which is followed immediately by corporal punishment hardly counts as
sin. It was a risk to be run. I lost out and now I must pay
for it. But then it is done with. Nothing remains of it, neither
remorse nor bitterness.

But the sin of disprizing love, of betraying love, *is* followed
by remorse, and that the most poignant. And it is a sin because the father and mother are the most natural image of
the Majesty of divine friendship.

THE VALUE OF THE HUMAN PERSON

Even if Brunschvicg does hold that science and ethics proceed from the same principle, he must agree with us at least in regard to certain facts. He must admit with us, for instance, the value of what we call a human conscience, and also of what is to him that bundle of corporeal appearance we call a child, wherein resides a conscience, even though this may still be in a dormant state. When a child is sick all agree — priest, nurse, and perhaps unbelieving doctor — that the preservation of the life of that little being, which may give no promise whatsoever of talent or extraordinary virtue, calls imperiously for all our self-sacrifice and absolute devotion. Suppose, on the other hand, that a philosopher, whose mind is teeming with clear and lofty ideas which he has never as yet been able to set down in writing, who has given the world just enough to make it eager to receive the whole of his thought, were to plunge into the water and be drowned in a futile attempt to save a drowning child, just any child whether he ever knew and loved it or not, would not all once more agree in praising his act? We could not but approve.[4]

Man, the human individual, is for us something sacred, and to lose one's life in such a service of love is to gain it. Of course, we must devote ourselves to society as well as to the individual members of it; but without this absolute value of the person, I fail to see how any group, no matter how large it may be, can claim my respect and love. In Kantian terminology, the group, to interest me, must be a "kingdom of ends." "Never consider humanity in yourself or in others as a mere means, but always as an end." The formula is true and Brunschvicg should agree with it, but it is heavy and abstract. It barely touches the truth. The Gospel is far clearer. The first Commandment is to love God, and the second is like unto

---

[4] The allusion is to the heroic death of Professor Hamelin.

the first: Thou shalt love thy neighbour as thyself. To love
God and to love one's neighbour is the same thing, the same
love. On this point also there must be agreement, for without
this participation of the human person in the Divine, what
meaning can we attach to ethics and morality?

We do not claim that this participation of the human
person in the divinity is the most evident thing in the world.
We must give proof of our good moral will, and the test consists in the fact that this divinity is too often hidden from us.
The fellow alongside of me in a railway train irks me by his
banality and apparent vulgarity and still more by his dis-
agreeableness. From the point of view of scientific positivist
reason, the value of the person strikes one as doubtful and
precarious. Is it a rational fact? And even supposing that there
is an instinct of love of man for man, that instinct is strongly
combatted by its contrary, the selfish individual instinct to
live one's own life. To love man, every man, whether he be a
criminal or an imbecile, of whatever race, colour, creed, something more is needed than mere natural instinct; *respect* is
needed to dominate external appearances and natural instincts: *Homo homini deus,* man becoming a god to man.

If we were to go by appearances, we should be led to believe in the mere chance or the futility of existence. Has the
existence of my neighbour any meaning? It is not the secret of
infinite worlds that is mysterious, that of the farthest stars (if
indeed there are any stars that are the farthest!), but that of
the "man on the train" who enters my life for the few brief
hours during which he sits beside me in the railway compart-
ment. What can his existence mean? A useless weight on the
earth, holding on to life with a blind instinct, like that of a
dog or of a gnat. But why? What possible reason can he have
for living?

The most disquieting problem that presents itself to who-
soever takes the trouble to reflect upon his own experience
and upon that of others in so far as he has access to it, is the
mystery of the waste, the unavailing effort, the futility that

appear to stamp the lives of the immense majority of human beings, of whom indeed, as it often seems, the most that can be said is that they were born, that they moved about awhile, and that they died. For one whose name survives in even the narrowest of chronicles how many thousands are there not of whom nothing at all is remembered, just because there is nothing at all to remember?[5]

But there can be no truly great man, no great or valid existence at all without this "unrational" faith in the importance of these seemingly unimportant and insignificant brethren, without this devotion to the many. Horace's satirical touch on the vanity of glory seems to me very poorly chosen: What remains of the exploits of Hannibal? What are they good for now? — To serve as the subject of schoolboys' exercises!

Ut pueris placeas et declamatio fias. But can there be any more desirable glory for us, either in life or after death, than that of making children happier? Children in general and each child in particular. That child is a little human being! His life is precious.

This respect, this *maxima reverentia* due to childhood, is not directed to the child as a child, but to the *man* who *is* already, and yet is, mysteriously, in the making. It is respect for the great human adventure of salvation or perdition, which is taking place within that child, of the struggle for the immortal soul that is his.

It must be obvious to all how greatly this respect excels mere humanitarianism. Considering the latter in itself, pure and simple, as a loyalty to the human species — a species, it would seem, that is somewhat privileged among the other species of animals — although we may concede it to be an abstract theory of progress, it is not an efficient doctrine of love, it is not fraternal, nor is it human. How can it see the *Os sublime* in the face of a leper? Humanitarianism preaches the suppression (by the gentlest of means, to be sure) of these

————

[5] Steuart: *Temples of Eternity* (Longmans, London).

"undesirables." To embrace the leper as did St. Francis, one must, in the words of Arnold Lunn, be not merely humanitarian, but "divinitarian." Such a one was St. Peter Claver who loved as his children, because he revered them as the children of God, the Negro slaves, the very lowest and most abandoned outcasts of humanity, to whom he devoted his life and labours.

But humanity, holy and divine by its participation in the Spirit, is not an empty idol. If it has an absolute worth, then its action, individual or social, also has an absolute worth. And from thence we can conclude to the value of devotion to a person or to a society, and to that work which we are to achieve: the formation of a society, a reign of minds.

Further, the value of humanity in action, working together to produce that action, entails the value of the milieu, the terrestrial, temporal conditions of the action. If man is divine and if God is in everything, everything is replete with the divine. We can't divide the universe into two parts, the one negative, excluding all value, the other having a positive value. We can't attribute a meaning to man in a world deprived of meaning. The sanctity of the moral law is bound up with the Socratic principle: the good and better is the reason for all things in the heavens and on earth.

Before we can speak of salvation and true conversion, we must first agree in accepting this first principle: that things have some value; that there is no fact pure and simple, devoid of all value, but rather all is value.

In brief. If man and human society have any value in themselves, that value must overflow into all human actions and into everything that conditions human activity; into the performance of the work and the materials used, in a word, into the sensible world. If what man does on the earth and what he makes of it has a real value and an eternal worth, then the earth also has its value by participation. It is a secondary value, to be sure, but a real value when viewed in the light of eternity.

THE VALUE OF TIME

There is a story told by Anatole France of a young Persian king who, on ascending the throne, asked the wise men of his kingdom to write him a complete history of Persia that he might find therein some lessons of wisdom in government. They spent ten years in writing their history. Little time enough, but it was spread over hundreds of rollers. The Prince, however, had little leisure so he asked for an abridgement. The first one they made for him was still too long for a man burdened with the cares of an Empire. A second version, in one volume this time, reached him on his deathbed. " 'Tis too late you come," he said to the old historian, the sole survivor of that scholarly company which had first undertaken the task. "But tell me, Father, before I die, something about the history of Persia." "Sire," the old man replied, "the history of the Persians and of the whole world can be briefly told: Men live, men die. There you have it all."

That seems to be the only thing that matters for the peripatetic. There are always men, just as the heavens always revolve. It is this unending succession which interests the savant. But the life of each individual, and of what he does in the world, the life of empires which come into being and end, what does all that matter since nothing remains of them?

Herodotus is more pathetic. Xerxes at Abydos, reviewing his huge army from the shore, rejoiced and said that he was glad at heart; but later he wept, and turning to his companion Artabanus, he said: "I weep because the thought has come to me that of these thousands of men not even one will be alive in a hundred years. So short is our life. For each one of us and for all, what is happening now will be the same as though it had never happened." "There is something still sadder," replied Artabanus; "even in this life, short as it is, there is not a single one of us, not even the happiest, who does not feel, not once but many times, that it would be better to be dead." "Very true," said Xerxes, "but let us not think about it and turn our minds to the fine projects we have in hand." Yes, let's make merry and only pretend to take things seriously. "The truth of the matter," added Artabanus, "is that God in His eternal beatitude is forever jealous of the joy of living and keeps it all for Himself."

Belief in the jealousy of the gods no longer exists in our day, but the opposition between time and eternity still exists. Whence, two alternatives are offered to the scientist: either to curse and defy the Eternal, return Him indifference for the indifference he attributes to Him, and love all passing things simply because they pass away — *Aimez ce que jamais on ne verra deux fois* — or to escape from time into the eternal, realising for oneself an eternity outside of time.

It would seem that even with this as a basic principle, one might keep the idea of a Providence and salvation of the soul, of a human and divine ethics. God would be the God of spirits. The time of life would have only a negative value as a time of trial. Every soul would be called upon to eternalise itself by cutting away from time and the past, from all that happens in time and passes away with time. The classic virtues would remain but would assume the guise of abstention and liberation. The highest virtue would be to play the game of life according to its rules, without however, allowing oneself to be captivated by it. Finally, the *Credo* would be to believe in nothing one does, to be afraid to lose oneself in wholehearted devotion to some cause, or to an interest which is not eternal; one's family, for instance, or one's country.

Theoretically this was the conclusion of all the ethical teaching of the ancients, for they were unable to discover the relation between time and eternity. Plato the disciple of Socrates, if not Plato the author of the *Laws*, believed in the value of souls outside time and in the reward for a life which jealously holds itself aloof from all temporal interest. The events of life, whatever they may be, are for each man a means of saving his soul; they are like dice, and the chance in the cast of the dice. But one is never attached to the dice for themselves. No one can make anything real out of the luckiest cast of the dice. In the same way it is impossible to make anything divine out of the stuff of time which passes away.

From this point of view nothing has a spiritual value save a man's own life, and that, not because of anything it may achieve in the way of something lasting, but for the simple fact of making use of days which do not last.

This philosophy of escape, being individualistic, cannot be the basis of a system of ethics. One of the first laws of ethics is to believe in the value of an action taken in a positive sense. The passing of time is the test of our faith in what remains in the divine and eternal works which, with the aid of God, we are capable of achieving. To be sure, one must not give up hope of making oneself eternal, but all the same, one must admit the eternal value of the good done in time. God can create nothing which does not bear the mark of the divine. Yet it is He who makes time and supports human action in time. It is He whose Providence runs through history.

"What is all that which is not eternal?" — But what is there that is not eternal, in the sense that it has not some value in eternity? Time without eternity would be a void. On the other hand, we can obtain an idea of eternity only by eternalising, so to speak, the values of time. An eternity with no relation to time, indifferent to time, and which does not perpetuate the values of time, is unintelligible for us. The eternal is independent of time, but we can conceive it only in the light of time.

Our life on earth and in time is an ever frustrated attempt to eternalise ourselves. Each instant of our lives is a synthesis of the past and the anticipated future. St. Augustine has well described the struggle of the soul to rescue itself from its dispersion, from its "times," the effort fully to possess oneself, and how this work of grasping and holding in check what is ever on the ebb and flow, can be accomplished only by directing oneself towards eternity or the Eternal, towards Him who is. We entrust to the Eternal the safekeeping of all goodness, of all that appears to pass away and disappear with time, our efforts to consecrate our life and to prevent it from passing away. But an eternity considered as indifferent to the values of time is the emptiest and the most unconsoling, the least divine of conceptions. It is the eternity of Spinoza — an eternity which accords no value to life in time.

Moral good has an absolute value and a divine worth. It is not lost, then; it is eternal. It is only in the making, of course, in the process of becoming, but this development is a process of eternalisation. The error is to contrast an abstract time with an abstract eternity. Real time is life and eternity is life, and no one has the right to oppose as two contradictories real time and real time. It is in the light of our own time, present and past, that we should conceive eternity. For eternity is a life which possesses all the reality and intensity of our life, without the dispersion. Incomprehensible and indefinable, but postulated by our effort to live, it is by experiencing life that we shall best conceive of eternity.

Mr. Taylor, whose learning and intellectual sympathies are so very wide, who knows the most recent modern writers as well as his Plato, to whom Einstein and the mechanics of waves are as familiar as the physics of the *Timaeus,* has this special claim to distinction among modern writers, that he has read and assimilated Scholasticism. He gives a good definition of eternity, that of Boetius, which the Scholastics adopted: *Interminabilis vitae tota simul et perfecta possessio,* the completely simultaneous and perfect possession of life interminable. It is, before all, life and not an axiom or system of axioms, and life cannot contradict life. It is not an impossibility that life, our life, should participate in eternity. If it comes from God it must participate in eternity. Eternity, then is a life, a divine life, infinitely rich and intense and freed from all the necessities imposed by matter, a life surpassing all life.

It depends on our good will to see to it that, so far as we are concerned, nothing should be lost, in spite of all appearances. We must believe that there is something of the eternal in time for us, wretched as we are, and for humanity in general; that the actions which we perform daily have an eternal importance; that all that is good and is worthy of love, abides; that the harmonised whole which I make of my actions, this work forgotten by men, the hymn which human ears hear no longer, abides.

But what of all that I was unable to do? What of all that I had planned to accomplish, simply and courageously, but for which time was wanting, as it usually is? Yes, true desires as well as actions, every courageous endeavour, will remain. "Not its mere semblance, but itself, the living thing, all beauty, all goodness, all power."

And of all the histories one single history is formed, the completion of which is guaranteed by the Eternal; and in this eternal termination all past values become present.

To believe in Eternity, then, is to believe in the value of my life and in the divinity of the moral law.

We all agree on saying "Eternity, Eternity," but we must choose an eternity which denies time, or one which creates and perpetuates it.

Xerxes should not have said: " 'Tis true, all will pass away and everything will be as if it had not been. Nevertheless let us enjoy ourselves at the royal game of conquering." But rather should he have said: "What I am undertaking, has it a human value or an eternal one? If it is human and a game of selfish ambition, nothing more will remain of it than my sin in doing it. Let us return to Susa and find some good to do which will last forever. It matters little whether I see the work completed; God can keep it in store for His eternal work."

It is not sufficient that our work should be done beneath the eyes of God for His sole look to eternalise them. If we go no further than that, we have nothing more than a Spinozan Eternity. His regard must not be indifferent and we ought to specify what sort of interest the Divinity takes in our time, in order to measure the importance which we ourselves should attach to it. It is here that the wisdom of Plato hesitates in a moment of pessimistic mistrust. What can our life be like in the eyes of the Eternal? 'Tis a mere game, an inconsequential amusement.

Our one purpose in life is to amuse the gods!

But even he does not stop there; he speaks to us later of a combat in which God is engaged as man's ally.

After all, one might still call life a game and lose nothing of its meaning. Understood correctly the "game," like happiness, is a serious matter. It is activity, no longer directed towards anything but itself. But it can be serious only if God takes part in the game. On His part it will be the present realisation of the eternal and the divine in time; on our part with the help of God and His grace, a progressive realisation, man being not simply an instrument, but a will, one with the will of God. It is a work that belongs both to man and to God, with the help of God.

"The Initiative of the Eternal" Taylor calls it. The Christian name for Initiative is preventive Grace.

The novelist Stevenson realised poignantly this initiative. He knew also our need for it and the answer to that need:

"And why not grace? Why not God's grace, Hay? . . . We walk upon it, we breathe it; we live and die by it; it makes the nails and axles of the universe; and a puppy in pyjamas prefers self-conceit!"

We need an ideal which, at the same time will be an efficient cause. The possibility of writing my history and developing my personality cannot come from myself alone, especially as I begin without knowing my end. This is revealed only little by little. *Nondum apparuit quid erimus.* Things are being done, and without my knowing the issue I must co-operate. My activity prepares the way for the appearance of a proximate ideal. Could it effect this without the help of this grace? I think not. I do not feel that I myself am master of this perpetual invention that is moral life. Moral life, the will to do good, not simply the wish or desire, implies the reality of "value." It is a paradox of an ideal which shall be the efficient cause as well as the final cause. How would man, if left to himself, ever conceive the idea of going beyond himself, unless he had faith in the ideal and unless he felt within himself an intimate, efficacious force of idealisation?

The word which best expresses this moral attitude is "faith." Especially since moral progress does not consist in the observation, ever more exact, of a code of conduct exactly defined in advance. The ideal is revealed in small portions and with more and more exigency. It is not exactly true to say that the road from vice to virtue is, of course, hard, but that once one has attained virtue, he is on level ground and progress is easy. One is never on level ground. We must always go up higher. Further and unsuspected heights reveal themselves as we advance, and their attraction is ever more irresistible. Each time we forget ourselves to run a glorious risk, there is a recompense, not only in the growth of personality but also in the call to a more complete, more generous abandonment, to sacrifices previously unsuspected.

I go forward, and I do not know where it is that I am going. I have light enough only for each day, for its evil and its possibilities for good. "Lead kindly Light. . . . One step is enough for me." And some goad keeps urging me to advance. But,

the attempt to walk that road simply in my own strength is as likely to be fatal to my moral being if I make it late as if I make it early. Morality itself, when taken in earnest, thus leads direct to the same problems about "grace" and "nature," "faith" and "works" with which we are familiar in the history of Christianity, the religion which stands supreme above all others in its "inwardness" and takes the thought of regeneration of the self from its center with unqualified seriousness.[6]

------

[6] *Faith of a Moralist*, p. 224.

CHAPTER SEVEN

RELIGION, PERSONAL SALVATION, AND HISTORY

CONTINUING THE THREAD OF THOUGHT BEGUN in the previous chapter, we shall here turn back for a moment and take up with Hocking the origin of the religious fact, its meaning for man and for society at large, and its significance for personal salvation and the progress of the human race. Our enquiry, we may state from the first, will lead to conclusions quite similar to his own on the questions of God's penetration into history, the obvious insufficiency of the God of the Scientists, and the antecedent plausibility of the God of Abraham.

Hocking is not an apologist. He studies as a fact the part played by the idea of God in human experience; or more exactly, the part played by religion in the life of man as an individual and as a member of society. He claims to show as a fact that religion, the religion of a transcendent God, is the source or the condition of those human values or ideas, be they true or false, which serve as reasons for living, and without which life is but a gamble, and the good and evil of human inclinations and unstable emotions are but relative and inconstant.

If life has a meaning, and if any reason can be advanced for a good life, then the meaning of life, and the reasons for living it well are religious. We have not to prove the existence of motives for leading a good life, nor even that religion, in the wide sense of the word, is necessary. The question asked at the beginning was: What religion can promise us the benefit we ask of it, namely, the exaltation of the human personality above self-centredness, and a true liberty of spirit? I shall sum up in a few words the points in Hocking's thesis which are concerned with the question before us and which have already been pointed out at the beginning.

Religion is the Mother of the arts and of life; it is itself a life, a force, and a source of riches greater than all the arts, and none of them can replace it. It offers us motives for living which nothing else can offer. It forms society and fashions or reveals to man a dignity that frees him from the tyranny of society. It creates a society of minds, making both the group and the individual depend directly on the providence, the wisdom, and the love of one God. Religion arranges this order in principle, but the order has continually to be rearranged and it is religion again that ensures its progress. It is a progressive creation.

If there is progress in history, it is certainly in the direction of the establishment of social union, and of the dignity of the individual; and this again is religion's work. Religion, as we now find it in the world, is a continued creation of human values. If religion were an exclusively social factor, if it were nothing else but the sacred regard which the individual is to have for the group and by which the latter subordinates completely the individual to itself, by that very fact the religious man would be the slave of society. He would cease to be a real person, and when the bond of religion slackened, as it eventually would, and the illusion of religion was dispelled, it is difficult to see how or where the individualist movement would end or how society could keep the authority and prestige necessary to be anything more than a precarious group of egoists.

Divine transcendence, upon which both the individual and society directly depend, as Hocking further argues, ensures both union and mutual independence. All the difficulties, however, have not been solved. How can the same religion be a religion of personal salvation and at the same time progressive social history? How do the salvation of the world and that of the individual coincide and form but one salvation? How, in fine, does religion give us in time the assurance of the good we hope to attain at the end of time, and the fulfilment of the history of God and man?

The contradiction is resolved in the actual working out of religion, and this is what Hocking shows us. Our good and our salvation, consist in adopting the divine idea of ourselves and of the world as it affects us, and accepting the universal nature of the plan. God saves souls and carries out in time an eternal plan. He makes the history of the world and of mankind, and out of the substance of this transitory world he realises, in some mysterious way, the eternal. But we may fail at first glance to see clearly how the plan of history is in harmony with the will of individual salvation, which comes first in the will of God. As far as we are concerned, is it not true that one of these is apparently in opposition to the other? Does not the precept of salvation seem to require us to withdraw from the world, from its works, its cares, and its plans which must look so far ahead? My salvation must be worked out in a short space of time, and immediately.

To save my soul is, indeed, my first and last care, and I cannot make my salvation depend upon a human ideal, and in particular not upon one whose realisation is so far off. In other words, we may say with Hocking, that religion must be immediate for the individual soul. Personal salvation cannot wait for the consummation of time. And yet, on the other hand, religion, in principle, is essentially social, and as it progresses it must tend to embrace, renew, and vivify the whole of humanity with a divine life.

The wonderful truth of the matter is, that religion itself, as we find it and as it is actually lived, quite simply resolves for us the seeming contradiction. The religious spirit, it is true, is one of recollection and of prayer, *solius cum solo,* but at

the same time it is creative. It is creative not merely in the
sense of being blindly and unconsciously fruitful and produc-
tive, or in following the example of others, but in the sense of
a conscious, wilful creation.

Ruskin gives us a striking and beautiful symbol of this personal salvation as it is closely linked up with the historical
work, or the individual's part in history, yet which nevertheless is realised here and now, without any waiting for the fulfilment of the work of society. It is that of the medieval cathedral, as seen in the ensemble and unity of the work, and the
detail of the sculptures:[1]

> It is perhaps the principal admirableness of the Gothic
> schools of architecture that they thus receive the results of
> the labor of inferior minds, and out of fragments full of
> imperfection and betraying that imperfection in every
> touch, indulgently raise up a stately and unaccusable whole.

The perfection of the whole consecrates and immortalises
the free work of the individual in its own immortality.

> Gaze upon the old cathedral front, where you have smiled
> so often at the fantastic ignorance of the old sculptors; ex-
> amine once more those ugly goblins and formless monsters
> and the stern statues, anatomiless and rigid; but do not
> mock them, for they are the signs of the life and liberty of
> every workman who struck the stone: a freedom of thought
> and rank in the scale of being, such as no laws, no charters,
> no charities can secure.

The heavenly city of Jerusalem is built of these living
stones.[2]

---

[1] Quoted by Arnold Lunn in *Now I See,* p. 57.

[2] Religion involves a present possession in some sort of the very objects
which the arts infinitely seek. Knowledge, for example, is an infinite
quest in the order of nature — and in it there is no absolute certainty,
but only a growing probability and approximation: but the religious soul
knows *now* — and that without losing interest in the slow movement of
science. Human brotherhood also is an infinite problem — men have to
be *made* brothers, and the whole of history is requisite to tell the tale of
achieving the end: but in religion men are already brothers and experience their brotherhood in the moment of common worship. So with
morality: in time my moral task will never be finished, for my imperfec-

The religious man is a creator, or perhaps it would be clearer to say that the creative and renovating will in man is the effect of divine intimacy. To tend towards the transcendent God is to be above material interests and necessities, and to withdraw from the world. We must pray in silence. Let him who wishes to converse *solus cum solo*, alone with God, retire to the desert, or else make a desert for himself in his own soul. But this life of prayer will not make us definitely disinterested in human affairs.

The Sage in the *Republic*, thoroughly captivated and entranced by the beatific vision of the Good, is only distracted from it by his duty of gratitude to the city and in order to fulfil his unpleasant task and duty for a fixed time — the job of being a Philosopher-King. And for Plotinus much more surely than for Plato, the forgetfulness of the world is definite, for it does not seem to them possible for us to think of the world, human history, mankind and God, all at once. It is not the same for the true mystic, however, and Hocking, as well as Bergson, thinks that, without leaving God, and looking at all things from the viewpoint of God, he should find in prayer itself his vocation to creativity.

And to begin with, one effect of prayer will be a taste for and a discovery of the divine in things. That is most important. The mystic, far from being continually in the abstract, can apprehend that which is real and concrete much less abstractedly than the supposedly practical man and the realist. The "practical" man makes use of things, but he does not and cannot love them for themselves or for what is ultimate and of divine origin in each of them. He sees in them only their utility for his immediate purpose, and they have no value for him save insofar as they are useful. But the mystic

---

tion is infinite and my progress by small degrees; but religion calls upon me to be perfect at once, even as God is perfect, and in religion somehow I am perfect. Religion is the present attainment in a single experience of those objects which in the course of nature are reached only at the end of infinite progression (*The Meaning of God in Human Experience*, p. 31, Yale U. Press).

(and the poet also at times, though quite unconsciously) has the sense of the actual value of a thing (and especially of a person) — of its freshness and of its beauty in the instant, an instant which does not pass and which is above time. He "holds heaven in a wild flower . . . and Eternity in an instant." A common, everyday sight strikes him as quite new and wonderful, a thing of inexhaustible wonder. Here lies the world-wide difference between Spinoza and the true mystic. To Spinoza, an instant is merely an instant of our life in time, a point, an imperceptible link in the chain of time. We do and feel at any given moment, whatever the inflexible mathematical chain of events in time makes us feel or do. It is an instant of the dreariest necessity. Not so with the mystic. His view of the object in the instant is no doubt partly relative to what goes before and partially determined by it, but not entirely. There is something in it that is original and wonderful, unaccountable, inexplicable in terms of time for it touches eternity — God's eternal instant.

We marvel at a sound, at a nuance of color, or a name, as if we saw or heard of it for the first time. Above all we marvel at a man, at a human gesture. Wonder is a gift of the mystic as it is of the philosopher, but here again we must distinguish. There is an intellectual rational wonder which is good, but is not as yet strictly speaking divine. It is the feeling of a contradiction, a problem to be solved, in the simplest of facts. This wonder is mingled rather with pleasure than with pain. It is the joy of a soul which finds a beautiful way of exercising itself and anticipates the pleasure of the exercise. This wonder is more spiritual and subjective when the object has no value save as the occasion of this moment of more intense intellectual life; it is a wonder of the curious, the searcher, of whom Aristotle is perhaps the best example.

Mystic wonder is different, and I do not say that there is no trace of it in Aristotle. It is an amazement and wonder at the concrete living object; astonishment and joy that it exists and exists as it is; contact with the singular existing reality, in its profound originality, in such a way that there is no longer any problem to solve. To make a problem out of it would be to reduce this originality to something already known, this living thing to something abstract, or in other words to destroy it completely. Whatever the object, and however humble, the feeling which it wakes in the mystic is analogous to that of Plato's lover before the face that suddenly recalls the divine Idea. He is drawn and held by respect. He all but falls down and adores it as a God.

"The more spiritual a man is, the more easily will he be able to distinguish the originality in each character." We might say also, and with more truth: the simpler, the more childlike and saintly we are, the more sensible are we to the divine novelty in things. As for our childhood, it is, alas, difficult for us to recall it. But a few indications would lead us to think that the first intellectual life of a child is a succession of these "wonderings" at the fact that things are, and that each is what it is. It is not a remembrance of immortality, but it is the divine light which enlightens every man that comes into this world and from which he has not yet been distracted by the cares of this world into which he has come.

This sense, or presentiment of the divine in things, may lead to prayer and union with the divine, it may also be the answer to prayer. What is certain is that the more direct and intimate union with God the mystic experience, *solius cum solo* does not destroy our interest in things, but rather turns it into love and a fruitful recreative power. We are made to participate in the interest God Himself has in the world, and to collaborate with Him in its creation. For creation, considered in the object, lasts throughout the centuries.

A pessimist may conceive the desire to remake this sad world, but he wants first to unmake it. The mystic is an optimist. "God saw that it was good." And he sees it with the eyes of God.

The Demiurge of the *Timeus* delights in the beauty of his work, the world, a work similar to a living, perfectly regulated watch; a definite work as far as possible, save for details which must be left to the ingenuity of the lesser gods. He, the Demi-urge, the Supreme God, may take His rest. The work of creating is finished. The world may and must now continue on its own.

But for the Almighty power of our God and His creative love, the work is ever new, ever to be done. And he who, by divine grace shares in that love, the religious and the mystic soul, wishes to perfect and not to destroy in order to remake. He now admires in the thing not alone the simple presence of the divine which has made its reality original, but also the divine intention and what both the thing, and the world in which it is, ought to be.

And this is not a mere inclination, but a real necessity of Divine Love and of salvation as well. The soul will only be saved if it abandons itself and loses itself in order to save and create; if it does its humble yet, since it is also divine, its great part, to advance divine history and its consummation. This history, which is a progress of spiritualisation with man as its center, has but one end: to humanise all that is not man and to divinise man and the society of men. What form will this progress take? We can at best catch but a glimpse of the very next stage of it; "it has not yet been made manifest." But we do know that it is in the direction of a union and a love of men, one for another; of a dignity and holy character and a respect for the individual. *Homo homini deus.*

"Thy Kingdom come." It is the history of the Kingdom of God, of the one true Society of souls. And he who will not work for it, let him not entertain any false hopes of an individual salvation. His personal salvation is closely linked up with this work of creation. And the mystic, he to whom it is granted to penetrate most deeply into intimacy with the living God, is also the most creative. First he renounces the world, for that is the price of divine intimacy. He then seeks God by prayer in solitude and by the rooting out of his passions, or by a purification of them that resembles death, by cutting himself

off from all love save the divine Love. And it is only then
that the creative force of religion bursts forth in him. Having
found God, and without leaving Him again, he is spurred
on to do God's work, to make the world like unto the image
of God.

The mystic experience tends of its nature to be prophetic.
It announces a victory yet to be gained, and it anticipates it.
It can only be sustained by turning oneself to the task of gain-
ing this victory. Any cult or religion which has no sanction
in the way of life which follows from it and which it determines, is false. This sanction must be twofold. First of all,
true religion, or true prayer, far from undermining the world
of other vital values, rather sustains and supports them. The
mystic on leaving his prayer, does not love the world less
because of his prayer. On the contrary, his love for men is
more intense, more intelligently human, for it is only the man
of prayer who finds the world really deserving of love. The
vision of God gives a reason for all the rational affections, the
devotions which, from a strictly rational point of view are
folly, such as self-sacrifice to the cause of our brethren in the
world, to the cause of one's country, or to any noble cause.

The man of prayer not only maintains and supports the
values, but he also creates them. And that is the second sanction. All beauty, says Plato, tends to reproduce itself. It pushes
ever on for more, for an original production. In the vision
of God there is a superabundance which makes him who sees
it turn, not towards the ancient, but towards the new. He
does not leave this vision and communication with God
simply freed from the old earthly trials, but even eager to
labour and to struggle. The edge of the blade, the will, is
sharpened; it is ready and impatient to begin its work of
making the world.

That is the answer to prayer. The mystic had turned towards the One, he turns back to the world of the many, which
is now more real and powerful for him than before. Divine
love, in answer to prayer, creates creative strength. The mystic

is at once both a prophet and a worker in this creation. Hocking speaks admirably of this prophetic and active attitude. He calls it the "prophetic consciousness."

> By the prophetic consciousness I do not mean a knowledge that something is to happen in the future, accomplished by forces beyond myself; I mean a knowledge that this act of mine which I now utter, is to succeed and hold its place in history. It is an assurance of the future and of all time as determined by my own individual will, embodied in my present action.[3]

Obviously, this assurance is an ideal, and so is not often attained. But the spirit of prophecy is essential to religion and religious activity. Without it history is condemned since it is beyond the sphere of justice and of reality. Without the possibility of the prophetic consciousness, this region of the historic future will always be for our wills a realm of chance, impenetrable and even hostile to the Spirit. This assurance of the prophetic consciousness is linked up with the idea of a dependence, but it pertains to a divine liberty, which is the substance of our own liberty. The human *fiat* of the believer is but one with the *fiat* of God. Alone, my will cannot claim for itself an individual creative power; it abandons hope. It is so evidently surpassed by the immensity of history. In other words, I have no choice but that of dependence. As a follower of Spinoza, I am overcome by the pressure of all the past weighing upon the instant. I can only escape from it by faith in a Love, Creator of both time and history, the author and support of my liberty, which calls for my acquiescence, my effective co-operation. God alone, Transcendent Will, gives a meaning to the moral law and ethics, to the moral effort of the individual and of society.

If we recognise frankly this liberating dependence, the origin of our hope and energy, I do not see what obstacle can be opposed to the recognition of God revealing Himself in history. If history is God's work, if all natural determinism,

---

[3] *Op. cit.*, p. 503.

the ensemble of physical laws, only frame the development of a world in the direction willed by God and whose end is divinisation, it does not seem impossible that God should insert Himself into history and manifest Himself therein, in order to mark for us its course and its divine end. On the contrary it is very probable that He should do just that and it is to be expected. Reason will never prove the necessity of this historic revelation, but it can never oppose it, save in virtue of its false postulate of mathematic fatalism. The world, says the disciple of Descartes, ought to be a problem of rational mechanics, so that reason might explain it entirely. But is such a right, assumed by mathematical reason to explain everything adequately, a first and absolute principle, or a gratuitous postulate? It is so far from being absolute, remarks Mr. Taylor, that a more recent and more enlightened science adopts the historical point of view of an unforeseeable future even in physics. Here I shall merely quote, without insisting on the point. This argument *ad hominem Cartesianum* is not necessary for my thesis.

If ancient science and philosophy have for their object the Unchangeable, or this image of the Unchangeable in time, which is the infallible repetition of the same events, modern science, freed by Carnot's principle from the superstition of the "equivalence of phenomena," has this sense of the "historical" in a much greater degree.

It is from the history of human life that they [the scientists] have drawn the conviction that the past does not recur, and when they make its non-recurrence into a corner-stone of their physics, they are definitely breaking through the old classical Platonic tradition of a purely geometric, natural world. We see exactly the same tendency to make physical science historical, in a way in which it could not be historical under the classical tradition, from Plato to Newton, in the anxiety of Dr. Whitehead to save natural philosophy from becoming flatly incredible by making the eminently historical concept of organism its foundation. Must we not say, in the light of such considerations, that the peculiarity which Celsus alleges as a reproach against the spirit of

Christianity, its insistence on a *muthos* which cannot be allegorized, is in fact its glory? What the complaint really means is that with Christianity there came, for the first time, into the Graeco-Roman world, a really adequate appreciation of individuality. We are still far from having done full justice in our philosophy and science to all the implications of this heightened sense of the reality of the individual, but we are on our way to do so. The historicising, if I may call it so, of the physical sciences, now apparently in process, is but one further step along the same road, which has led, in our moral social and religious thinking, to the conquest of the great conception, so imperfectly grasped in ancient philosophy, of personality in God and man.

The particular point to which I would draw the attention at present is this. All the various tendencies, so familiar to us in the intellectual life of our age, which are most hostile to the recognition of the historical as an indispensable element in religion, the disparagement as merely temporal and accidental of everything in the positive religions which resists reduction to positions of general metaphysics, the hardly concealed desire of some, even among our theologians [Anglican] to obliterate the distinctions between a faith like Christianity and the kind of religion possible to a Neo-Platonic Philosopher, the anxiety of metaphysicians of various schools to interpret the affirmations of all positive religions as no more than figurative expressions of some vague principle of "conservation of values," all are, if we come to reflect, only forms of the old protest against "the myth which refuses to be allegorized." And this means that they spring from inability to adjust one's mind to the characteristically modern habit of thinking historically, as one sees, in fact, quite plainly in the efforts of the small minority who "follow the argument wherever it leads," to discard even the bare facts of the actual existence of a personal founder of Christianity.[4]

---

[4] *Faith of a Moralist*, Vol. II, p. 330 (The Macmillan Co.).

CHAPTER EIGHT

CONCLUSION: "GIVE US GOD!"

CANON GUY ROGERS, IN HIS EXCELLENT LITTLE
book in the *Return to God*[1] series, records an anecdote which
he attributes to George Borrows, author of *Wild Wales*. Near
the town of Chester, Borrows fell in with some wandering
tinkers who insisted on taking him for a minister and talking
to him about their souls. At the end of the conversation they
said to him: "O sir, give us comfort in some shape or other,
either as priest or minister; Give us God! Give us God!"

"I am neither priest nor minister," replied Borrows, "and
can only say: 'Lord have mercy upon you.'" Then getting up
he flung the children some money and departed. "We do not
want your money, sir," screamed the woman after him; "we
have plenty of money. Give us God! Give us God! . . ."

The Canon goes on to say that this need of God has never
been so keenly felt as at the present time. "Give us God!"
This is the demand that the world is making today with insistence and even with violence, of its accredited teachers.
The violent reactions in certain quarters against religion, are
really reactions against the fraudulent manipulation of God
by interested parties. The bitter hatred is that of the betrayed
and outraged lover. And this attitude is no longer what it
appeared to be to Matthew Arnold and those of his day, "a

---

[1] Canon T. Guy Rogers, *The Return to God* (London, Arthur Barker).

gentle melancholy, expectant of defeat"; it is a firm demand that will not be put off without an answer. The time for poetic melancholy has passed. "There is nothing wistful about the ordinary man. In his view the situation needs radical treatment. God for him is the alternative to chaos. God is the eternal affirmation in a world of doubt."

The gypsy woman in the story, the philosopher, and the modern "ordinary man," all have that same need of some divine reason for living, some reason which will deliver them from the oppressive conditions of temporal existence and justify and fortify human activity in giving it a real end above and beyond time. They need the assurance that nothing of the good they do in time is lost, that Eternity consecrates and conserves the brotherhood of man, purified and divinised, with all that it accomplishes. Man needs a God who is Spirit, to inspire him to good works, a God who is present and whom he will be sure to find at the end of life.

How can rationalistic and tyrannical reason, ignorant as it is of all Good, be that God?

We need a living transcendence, a Will with which our own can be kept in accord, a God whom we can love with a love that is free and voluntary. To love without any idea of return, to love what one knows to be absolute insensibility, because divinity is supposed to be insensible by right, that is a vital contradiction. It is to converse with someone who cannot hear, and who cannot reply precisely because he cannot hear. This God that we need must be at the same time supreme. He must be all things and above all things. Nothing can limit Him in any way, and if He is creative love, nothing can restrict His creative activity or His Love, neither in any particular nor in the whole. And so He is the Creator of time and of history. Nothing of what He creates is indifferent. Everything enters, everything must enter, into this divine work of divinisation.

What prerogative of the Divinity of this God, who is at one and the same time so distant and so near, and who is

immanent in history — what prerogative would forbid Him
while He is fashioning history, to manifest Himself in some
place and at some certain time which His Liberty might
choose? What impossibility is there on the part of God that
there be prophets and a prophetic people? What impossibility
that there be a Man so completely possessed by the Divine
Principle that He is not Himself insofar as He is man, but
God, the Son of God?

In reality there is nothing to argue against it, and yet
reason resists; that limited reason that wants to explain everything, to reduce everything to rational necessity, to facts entirely explicable, to demonstrable propositions; Reason, the
enemy of all mystery and of all liberty whose workings cannot
be accurately foretold, even though that liberty be the Divine
Liberty. We must admit the fact of this prejudice, which is
neither specifically Hellenistic nor Cartesian nor Spinozan,
but simply human. If there is a free intervention in history
on the part of God, we must believe the evidence of that intervention, we must have faith. And this same faith, reasonable
as it is, is nevertheless beyond reason, and troubles it always.
The firmest belief does not lessen the need of remaking the
real rationally.

But it is one and the same intelligence which, realising its
own limits, calls for a revelation. Yet it is amazed to find
itself outstripped by its own exigencies. It is torn within itself.
It calls imperiously for the divine, and yet it would like first
to be able to explain it, to rationalise it, that is to say, to
empty it of its divinity; it would like to show the rational
necessity, the antecedent demonstrability, not only of the
existence of God and of the divine attributes, but of all the
proceedings of the divine Will; it would like to submit the
Divine entirely to rational determinism. It would rob it, in
other words, of its own divine self-determination.

But would you have us believe that Providence would bind
itself to one place and to one person? So this narrow Reason
enquires. God of Abraham! Why Abraham and not Aristides

or Numa, or better still Socrates? Why was the promise made exclusively to him? Jesus of Nazareth! Why Nazareth among all the cities and towns of the world? Or even, why our insignificant planet, more lost in stellar space than Nazareth in the Greco-Roman world? And to speak of Jerusalem or Rome as privileged cities is to make reason even more suspicious. There is no human reason why the Divine should appear in Nazareth; there are too many human reasons why Jerusalem or Rome should be a city divinely chosen. It is a scandal that the vicar of Christ should be Peter, a fisherman of Galilee, and it is a scandal that he should be Bishop of Rome. In fine, any *particular* will or providence would seem to be unworthy of God.

As soon as the Divine is *localised* it becomes suspect. "Don't try to give us your Christ as a fact of history," said Celsus to the Christians. The modern rationalist cries: "Anthropomorphism!" And indeed, God does become man! The Word is made Flesh. But when we speak of "Providence" and "Creative Love" we are already speaking anthropomorphically, as well as when we speak of divine solicitude for humanity or for a single soul. But to restrain this interest that God takes in humanity, the humanity which He has created, is to anthropomorphise even more. There is nothing so wretchedly anthropomorphic as the God of "general Providence," who must be so sparing with miracles. This God would be like the praetor, who could not be bothered with petty details. *De minimis non curat praetor.* And so the divine ideas would be general concepts, abstract laws, as far removed as possible from concrete reality. And yet God has created the real in all its complexity and singular details, as well as in its whole. The least improper thing we can say of Him is that His Thought, like His Creation, is at the same time of every detail and of the whole.

That is true unless, again, we are to free God entirely from all anthropomorphic Providence and make Him ignorant of all that is being done, of all that is. And this precisely must be the natural conclusion and consequence of rationalistic idealism. We must insist again on that point, namely, that there is no middle course between the God of human science, who ignores, or is just ignorant of, the world, and the God of Abraham who makes and saves and divinises history.

A religion which refuses to be "historic" is inefficacious, because it is too abstract, too human. Everything belongs to God, everything proceeds from Him, everything is divine, History as well as science. How then can science, or a scientist in the name of science, set up its God as a God necessarily opposed to the God of History?

Reason, they tell us, must be true to itself and admit of no object of worship, no God that is *unscientific*. History, what happened once and can never happen again, can lay no claim to scientific or rational recognition, for science is of the universal, since it can be determined and accurately anticipated by rational experiences and experiments.

The scientist is free, of course, to call "Science" the rational investigation of natural laws in the domain of inert matter. But if we mean by "Science" what is most *real* and most interesting theoretically and practically to the mind of man, we must say that the proper study of man is man — and man as a free agent working out his destiny and the destiny of the race. In that case science is history.

Compared with this actuality, science, physical science, is of the abstract and unreal and merely provides a framework and the conditions for the realisation of living reality. Uniformity and absolute laws, the object of physical science, belong to inert matter before the apparition of life. Life, even in its lowest forms, means spontaneity and consequently a certain degree of imprevisibility. And what is spontaneous and imprevisible is also the most interesting and most real.

The object of history is man, actually existing, and man in the making; the work of his liberty is to realise a perfect state, individual and social; the evolution of this work implies progress towards the goal, and occasional regression. But for

the achievement of this same work and the arrival of mankind
at this goal, there is needed a unity of purpose, independent
of the many and conflicting views of men, and yet immanent
in them and using them and their free efforts to make them
converge towards the one end — God in history! And hence
man's natural anticipation of and wish for a divine manifestation in the course of time, at any moment chosen by God, to
show us whither we are bound, and to help the infirm will and
the wavering mind. Any messenger bringing us the words of
eternal life must be rationally welcome. Welcoming the messenger of eternity will be *rationabile obsequium,* though man
has no right to that revelation and the liberty of God's gift
remains unimpaired.

Diffident and sceptical minds (and we must not forget that
diffidence and scepticism are weaknesses!) will often raise the
following objection, which they think unanswerable: "There
are too many such messages, divers and conflicting. All are
impostures but one, if even one, and how can we know that
one?" And proud and weak and lazy minds find here an
excuse for resting in unbelief. "All prophets are deceivers or
self-deceived."

But is it true that there are many strictly or truly historical
systems of religion, in which the historical fact itself is an
essential part of the message? One may rightly contend that
there is only one, the Religion of Christ. The originality, the
unique historical character of Jesus and His message has been
clearly shown in a capital passage of an important book on
the History of Religions by Rousselot and Huby:

> "A dispute about one Jesus, deceased, whom Paul affirmed
> to be alive. . . ." Here is what, in the year 60, a Roman
> official could observe about the Religion of Christ. Many
> abstract definitions have been given since of the essence of
> Christianity, but none comes so close to the core of the
> matter as the brief description of Porcius Festus. Christian
> belief is founded on a fact, the life of Jesus; and Christians
> today, as of old, are those who believe in the life of Christ,
> in Christ still living.

And in this precisely does the unique character of our religion consist. Other religions call themselves revealed religions, but all, even the Jewish Religion, lack that characteristic of a revelation embodied in a person and a life, essentially bound up with that life, the Religion of a Man who gives himself out not merely as a messenger of justice and truth, but as being Himself living Truth and living Justice.

There have been historical founders of religions whom the people in their time could hear with their ears, touch with their hands, but none of those prophets, or preachers, Mohammed, Buddha, Zoroaster, has proposed his own self as the direct object of belief. They all preached a doctrine with no essential relation to their own person. Whether they started new currents of religious thought or simply, as usually happened, organized and gave a common aim to pre-existing tendencies, the movement they originated had not themselves for its end. Jesus is the one Master who gives Himself as the object of our faith. He is the author of it and the finisher as well (Hebr. XII:2). He is in the foundation of the building, as the cornerstone; and on the pinnacle, as the God to be adored. Mohammed, Zoroaster and Buddha were *merely* historical personages. They flourished in their times as Plato and Aristotle in theirs. What remains of them and still exerts an influence, is only the remembrance of their writings. Jesus Christ is much more than an historical hero, a great man. He is both immanent in the course of history by His continuous action in His Church, visible and invisible, and transcendent, established above the stream of time, He is Life itself ever present.

The History of the Christian Religion means the History of Christ living in the Church.

"The God of Abraham and the God of Jesus" (the historical meaning and value of Judaism being the expectancy of Jesus and the preparation for His coming), Christ, the Son of God, claims our allegiance, our faith in His advent, death, resurrection, and actual life with us to the end of the world.

But what preacher, what new Paul, has the merest chance of making a modern audience accept such a God? We answer that whoever the preacher be, whatever his gifts, the soul will meet him halfway; for there is many a modern soul secretly hungering after God, and which refuses to be satisfied by a mere abstract and rational deity, the work of human reason, a God subject to human reason, bereft of liberty and life. The soul wants a God of the heart and soul, and yet a sovereign God, almighty, transcendent, and immanent. The only belief that is likely to satisfy it is the dogma of the Man-God, God freely assuming and taking to Himself our human nature, Christ who dies on the Cross, who, risen from the dead, can die no more; Christ living in each Christian soul, calling her to the participation in His life and passion, and consequently to personal salvation, Christ living in the Church and in her and through her, realising the Kingdom of God.

The statement "Christ is God," says Mr. F. J. Sheed in a very penetrating essay on the Modern Attitude Towards God, is in form a statement about Christ; and indeed it tells us an enormous fact about Christ. But in practical living fact it tells us still more about God. To bring what we know of God to the understanding of Our Lord is fruitful; but to bring what we know of Our Lord to the understanding of God is something immeasurable and altogether revolutionary.

It is certain that if man does not get his idea of God through Christ, it will not be a living idea. And any effort to bring men back to God save through Christ is doomed to sterility. Philosophy cannot do it; it can help, and its help is essential: but of itself it cannot set the inert mass in motion towards God: only the Gospel can do that.[2]

Let us conclude: As regards the mystery of God, men can be divided into three classes: (1) Those who, bereft of dogmatic belief, knowing of no divine revelation or message, are nevertheless hungering and thirsting after some divine interpretation of human life, after the Good, after reasons that will make life worth living, all those who, in divers languages, call upon the unknown God. . . . "Give us God! Give us God!" (2) The great number of people of the present day who are indifferent, bent on living and enjoying the instant, asking for nothing more than actual bodily comfort and rec-

---

[2] F. J. Sheed, "The Modern Attitude to God," in *God* [Cambridge Papers], edited by E. Lattey, S.J. (Burns, Oates and Washbourne).

reation, who have no cares for the distant future or for any
work to be achieved; people for whom the world is in vain
and who live in vain, aimlessly and contentedly, how many
and for how long, God only knows. To them applies what
Mr. Joad has to say of the modern man:

> He has won powers fit for the gods, and brings to their
> employment the mentality of a schoolboy. Notwithstanding
> his mastery of the secrets of nature, there is one secret, it
> may be, that still escapes him, the secret of how to live: "We
> are taught to fly in the air like birds and to swim in the
> water like fishes, but how to live on earth we do not know."

(3) And finally there are those who believe in Christ and His
Church. You may find among these a man poor, fallible, weak;
often unequal to his privilege, unfaithful to the divine ideal;
he may recognise and admire and envy in many an unbeliever
of good faith, certain virtues, truly Christian virtues, which
are wanting in himself. But in his misery he can at least bear
witness to a divine experience. He is aware of a mystery of
the closest divine intimacy and friendship in his inmost soul,
and he knows that the deepest and dearest mystery is to him
the very reality of that intimate union; that when he is at
his best his religion is not merely a part but the whole of his
life. It has for centre the living Mediator Jesus Christ. If he
happens to be tempted and to waver in his faith he has only
to turn to the invisible Presence and say as Peter: "O Lord,
to whom can we go? Thou alone hast the words of eternal
life!" He has the certitude that without such a faith all is in
vain and human life is in vain. What makes him sure and
stable in his religion and what urges him to communicate
and spread the message of salvation, is the belief in the anticipated enjoyment of the fulness of life.

MEANING OF THE WORD "RELIGION"

THE FRENCH DICTIONARY OF PHILOSOPHY,[1] GIVES first and foremost a descriptive definition of religion according to its constituent elements. The elements of this specifically human and social fact, which we have agreed to call *Religion,* are described there as belief in a supernatural order or object, and further as the practice of an ensemble of social rites deemed efficacious for entering into relationship with this supernatural reality. "Supernatural" here signifies that which surpasses and dominates the life and experience attainable by natural means.

One may speak also of an interior, personal religion. By that is understood the spirit in which each one observes the rites directed by him towards a supernatural object, the manner of his belief in it, and the greater or less intensity of this belief.

What is called Natural Religion — the rational remainder of positive religions — is certainly not a primitive fact. One might well ask how this really differs from a philosophical treatise on God and His attributes. Such, for instance, was the religion of Voltaire. The only real life possessed by a doctrine of this kind consists in its hostility toward all positive religion. One wonders how far modern rationalism, when it declares itself religious, differs from this. Even M. Brunschvicg,

---

[1] *Vocabulaire de Philosophie.*

were he asked to approve of such a religion, would most probably reply: "The religion I preach is by no means this impoverished eclecticism. It is rather the sublimation of positive religion, at least in its loftiest and purest form; it is the religion of Jesus, from which it rejects the miraculous — which is merely human — and of which it preserves all that is spiritual and divine as well as all its moral efficacy."

Does this natural religion, we may further question, preserve the distinction to be observed between the two orders of reality the acceptance of which appears to Eucken even more essential than a belief in God? With the concept of that world which immediately surrounds us he contrasts another sort of existence, a new preternatural order, which is for him essential and indispensable to religion under all its aspects. In other words, the whole of reality is divided by him into different realms and different worlds.

Would a religion of pure immanence admit this distinction? In a sense, yes. Thus Brunschvicg apparently contrasts the scientific and divine orders on the one hand, with the nonrational order of facts on the other, the divine pursuing indefinitely its work of conquering and absorbing the nonrational.

In the Dictionary of Philosophy already referred to, under the word "Religion," occurs a statement by Blondel which expresses admirably what we hold as essential to the idea of a living religion:

> One cannot, without misunderstanding the original and truly specific element of religion, reduce it either to a social institution or to an individual system of opinions, beliefs and rites, or even to a compound of personal initiatives and collective reactions having God as their object. For that to which the believer attaches himself as the essential of his faith is not an *object*, idea or force, of which he might freely dispose since he himself has formed it or gotten possession of it. It is rather a *subject*, a being endowed not only with life and a will, but in addition mysterious and inaccessible to the natural grasp of our thought and action, revealing himself only as a favor by the testimony he gives of

himself and of his own transcendence, through written revelation, or by prescribing dogmas and practices which put
within our reach his very incommunicability. Whence we
have the essentially religious idea of a tradition which trans-
mits the revelation and the covenant of alliance as a sacred
trust. The social or individual element is there, but subordinated, as a means, or a material element. It is not the
formal element of religion. In consequence the religion
called natural is only a belated, artificial and denatured
extract when considered as something positive, in so far as
it believes itself penetrated with supernatural elements. And
whatever the deviations or inconsistencies may be which
turn it either toward superstition and magic, or toward an
ideological symbolism, or toward "statolatry," it is important to disengage in its original and logical purity the dis-
tinctive trait of religion, for which the philosophical explanations (be they psychological, metaphysical, or sociological)
do not suffice (p. 704).

Only such a religion, we believe, can raise man above himself and unite men among themselves without constraint. But
that is precisely what we must prove. A definition by "effects"
is the only one that has any likelihood of proving acceptable
to everybody.

If every religion up till the present has been of a social
nature, it may be asked whether this character is essential.
The rationalist, as we know, divests himself of rites and con-
ventions and social restrictions, as well as of the control of a
transcendent Being. Of the social reality he wishes to retain
only the psychological element, which is merely human and
individual. In what, then, does psychological religious reality
consist? Leuba in an appendix to his *Psychological Study of
Religion* gives a long series of quite varied definitions. Many
are alike in the postulate of that transcendence which rationalism wishes to abolish. To quote but two of these:

> *Spencer:* Religion is the belief in the all-powerful Un-
> knowable who reveals himself in all that is knowable.
> Avowal and worship of this mystery, the cause of all that
> appears.
> *Romanes:* Religion has as its object the principle or
> principles of things, and this principle is necessarily known
> as intelligent and personal.

Such definitions do not suit a rationalism which would at the same time be pure, exclusive of all authority, superior to reason, and yet religious. Transcendence on the part of the divine would bring reason into subjection, whereas, according to the rationalistic view, the religious idea or the religious sentiment must above all be free.

The definition of A. Ritschl is one of the most interesting in that it unites — whether logically or not — the freedom of the mind and the transcendence of the divine. Religion, he says, is the belief in a spiritual power which dominates the world and which guarantees our spiritual independence with regard to the limitations of nature and society. We have here a submission that liberates, a subordination rendered to a power both dominating and freeing. Perhaps rationalism could succeed in interpreting and transposing this definition.

Still other formulas might be mentioned which are more disengaged from the requirements of religious common sense or simply more vague. By some, indeed, every metaphysical emotion is captioned religion. We know that for Schleiermacher religion does not belong either to the domain of action or of thought. It is neither morality nor knowledge. It is the indefinable sense of the All, of a unity which is God. Our rationalist cannot content himself with a simple emotion without objective reason. Nor will he admit — at least Brunschvicg will not admit — the definition of McTaggart nor his optimistic postulate: "Emotion resulting from the conviction of a harmony between ourselves and the world."

More acceptable from the rationalistic and antitranscendental viewpoint, but too vague, is the definition of religion given by Hegel: "Knowledge that the finite mind has of its nature as infinite mind"; and that of Caird: "Our ultimate attitude towards the world, consciousness of some divine power of unity."

From these quotations two characteristics may be selected which I believe everyone will recognise as belonging to the religious sense, namely: exaltation and liberation.

The least that religion can imply is a sense of the absolute and the infinite which exalts the spirit and frees it from the constraints and limits of the life of phenomena, whether or not this infinite be conceived as transcendent. But even those who hold a religion of pure and simple immanence must admit what Eucken says in the passage already alluded to:

> An essential and indispensable element of religion under all its forms is that it stands in contrast with the world immediately surrounding us, being another sort of existence, a new preternatural order, and that it divides the whole of reality into different realms and worlds. Without the duality of the world, without the prospect of a new sort of being, religion is no more than an empty word.

Even though no reference should be made in such descriptions to transcendence in the true sense of the word, there is nevertheless in religious experience the idea and the sense of a superior order, and there is further an object, substance, or mode of being which at present surpasses our understanding and which we call God or divine. The terms, "a Beyond" or "a Superior Order," appear to be almost synonymous with transcendence, but the object of religious rationalism is to interiorise within ourselves entirely this first and provisory notion of transcendence and finally to suppress it.

To throw as much light as possible on this preliminary question let us consider two opposite interpretations of the religious sense. One is that of W. E. Hocking in an article entitled, "Les Principes de la Methode en Philosophie Religieuse" (*Revue de Metaphysique et de Morale,* 1922, p. 431). The other, by Bertrand Russell, appeared in the *Hibbert Journal,* October, 1912.

To begin with, it was Durkheim who remarked that religion is born of social rites. Yet would not these rites in themselves be already the religion which he is trying to explain, or could they not be conceived as the expression and the spontaneous sign of the primitive instinctive sentiment or belief?

Hocking, in search of the essence of religion, also starts

from the rite. This rite, or ensemble of rites — the cult, its regulated gestures, its processions — are placed by him under the head of relaxation. It thus is conceived of as an activity without any ulterior motive. Following the lead of Plato we might say that it is a game, but the most noble and the most serious of games, more serious than anything else we can do. A game agreeable to God and to men, the children of the gods. It is thus that the Greek city understood it. All social activity tended towards the leisure of peace; and the proper activity of peace consisted in such games in honour of the gods. But these Platonic considerations are parenthetical on our part. Hocking tells us simply that the cult gives birth to all the arts. Religion is "the mother of the arts." But we have not yet defined the meaning of this, for religion is not, as one might believe, the first of the arts, nor yet is it a blending of all the arts, where in a progressive sequence each secures its proper place — in some such way as the philosophy of a Presocratic was conceived as a blending of all knowledge and of all sciences vaguely glimpsed, each obtaining its autonomy in its own proper turn.

Cult has its specific functions with regard to nature and the forces of nature. It is not born from the fear of these tyrannical, inevitable forces, as has too often been said since the time of Epicurus. On the contrary, it is the affirmation of a power higher than the apparent necessity of nature, the affirmation of a power "conceived of as freedom, as free and making free." Psychological energy, when subjected to the necessities of nature, tends to decline from liberty to mechanistic determinism; the religious spirit is the tendency opposed to this degradation. Cult opposes religious habits of mind to combat others more subservient; it thus frees us.

As a social function, religion also frees us, or tends to free us, from a tyranny which society without religion is ever inclined to exercise upon the individual. It destroys that opposition which exists in human nature between the social instinct, on the one hand, and the tendency towards isolation on the other — a tendency that passes from social intercourse to independent solitude, from objectivity to exclusive individualism. In clearer terms, religion harmonises the sympathy or fellow feeling which is the postulate of social life, with the liberty or independence which is the postulate of individual life. How does it accomplish this? In setting before both society and the individual an object of veneration which surpasses them alike. Thus the function of cult is not to adjust differences but to bring adverse elements into communion with an object of mutual respect.

In this way cult and religion exercise their beneficent power on the individual and society. Together they contribute to the realisation of a more perfect society, built on mutual assistance and a community of interests, in which the unity achieved is permanent and brings freedom instead of servitude. If religion can dissolve social antinomies the reason is because it is independent of society, and, as Aristotle would say, has priority and precedence of right. Its social functions are not the *raison d'être* of religion. On the contrary, these social functions have a suprasocial and suprahuman object, an object that is strictly speaking religious, namely, God. Cult is the activity of adoration, and "the only justification of the act of adoration is the existence of an object of adoration." Adoration is of the very essence of religion. And this adoration is not a matter of lessened energy, simple resignation, fear, or submission, but a life "lived intensely," a life exultant and joyous.

A certain sociologist, admitting the originality of the religious fact and the good it has done, thus draws his own conclusions:

> It [religion] is a social fact, born in society and conditioned by it. The God adored symbolizes society, a symbolization necessary for the infancy of a people. Nothing, therefore, prevents us from keeping religion with its benefits, and even its rites, feasts, and games, so long as we define their true object — society, or better still, humanity.

This effort would be in vain, since its postulate is false. A living and sincere cult is not content with a metaphor. It will have no God that is mortal, no God that is merely a human reality. The unity of society, without doubt, is not imaginary, but it is derivative, it comes from elsewhere. Its unification must result from the movement of all towards a being that is superior and distinct. The unity of the social group is wrought through the medium of a profounder unity, the unity in an object of common adoration.

The object of the religious cult is extrapsychological and extrasocial, it must be truly adorable, it must deserve to be adored. It must have a power and a value that compel us to reverence it and to bow down before it. And nevertheless, to adore God, to serve God, is joy and freedom. These words are dissonant to the ears of our rationalists, filled with enthusiasm over their interior "God," which is nothing more than the interiorisation of the mind to itself. But do not pretend, says Hocking, to keep the benefits of religion without that objective God, real and transcendent, who is adored in the strict sense of adoration, and before whom one bows down in humility: "Either there is a metaphysical object of the cult, that is to say, a God, or else religion with its derived functions must disappear."

I go no farther here than to present the thought of a philosopher, a theologian, and a sociologist. If I had to judge it, I would certainly retain all that is positive in it. But I would add to it what there is of truth in the verse:

Primus in orbe deos fecit timor

that is to say, an element of fear, correlative with adoration and love, made men turn to "the gods." So, then, according to Hocking, the essence of the religious sense is adoration of a God superior to nature, to the individual, to society; superior to everything whose nature is to enslave us — a God, therefore, transcendent and all-powerful, a liberator. That, and the joy and sense of freedom in the adoration of him, constitute religion.

INDEX

Act of Potentiality, in Aristotle, 29
Aeschylus, purpose of, 16
Altruism, 103 ff.
Aristotle, 25 ff.; idea of eternity of
world in, 29; idea of God in, 26
f.; on presence of gods, 12
Arnold, Matthew, x
Augustine, St., 2

Belief, in God, reasons for, 99 f.;
necessity of, in God, to moral
man, 100 f.
Benn, A. W., on Aeschylean drama,
16
Bergson, Henri, on mysticism of
Greek philosophy, 44; on Spinozan intuition, 65
Blondel, quoted on religion, 154 f.
Bolshevism, vii
Bréhier, Emile, 1, 4; on Greek
philosophy, 18
Brunschvicg, L., ix; the god of,
viii; on religion and rationalism,
xi ff.

Catholicism and Hellenism, ix
Conscience, moral, sin, and law, 115
ff.
Cosmos, in system of Socrates, 18 f.
Cult, functions of, 158

Dogma, in Russell's religion, 81 f.
Drama, Greek, idea of sin in, 13

Epicureanism, 31; in doctrine of
Spinoza, 53; rationalism of, 32 f.
Epicurus, 30 ff.
Eternity, meaning of, 125 ff.
Ethics, in Spinoza's *Short Treatise*,
63 ff.; of Spinozan religion, 57 ff.

Eucken, on religion, 157
Euripides, rationalist, 18

Fathers, Greek, 2
Fichte, on reality of world, 108
France, Anatole, 124
Freeman's religion, impartiality in,
77, 80 ff.
Freeman's worship, 70, 71 ff.

God, and history, 108 ff.; in the
religion of Wells, 84 ff.; in Spinozan system, 45; modern need for,
143 ff.; necessity of belief in, to
moral man, 100 f.; origin of, in
Wells, 91 f.; polytheism does not
exclude idea of One, 10 f.; rationalistic idea of, xi; reasons for
belief in, 99 f.; unreal, of Bertrand Russell, 72
Gods, mystery of, 11; presence of,
Aristotle on, 12; presence of,
Heraclitus on, 12
Good, immortal, in Spinoza's
thought, 46 f.
Gospel, and the Greek mind, 8 f.
Greek fathers, representatives of
Greek culture, 2
Greek mind, and Gospel, 8 f.; reli-
gious, 18

Happiness, judgment of, in Greek
view, 10
Hellenic culture and rationalism,
8 ff.
Hellenism, and the Church, ix;
spirit of, xiii
Heraclitus, on presence of gods, 12
History, God and, 108 ff.; religion,
personal salvation, 131 ff.

Hocking, W. E., 112, 131 ff., 157 f.; on "prophetic consciousness," 140

Humanitarianism, 122 f.

Impartiality, in Russell's religion, 77, 80 ff.

Infinity, Russell's worship of, 76 ff.

Justice and injustice in Greek mind, 13 ff.

King, the invisible, of Wells, 84 ff.

Law, moral conscience and sin, 115 ff.

Leuba, on psychological religion, 155

Liturgy, pagan, norm of spirit, 10

Logos, in stoicism, 34

Love, in Spinoza's system, 46 f., 50, 54; in system of Plotinus, 41 ff.

Man, in Spinozan system, 50

Mystic sense, Russell's definition of, 170 f.

Mythology, in system of Socrates, 20

Natural religion, 153 f.

Naturalism, 11 ff.

Neoplatonism, 39 ff.

Paganism, Greek, 9

Paul, St., and Greek thought, viii

Person, human, value of, 120

Pessimism, in paganism, 10

Peter Claver, St., 123

Philosophy, Christian, 6 f.; difference between, and science, 99; Greek, and rationalism, 18

Plato, 20 ff.; and idea of sin, 24; as moralist, 23; as politician, 22 f.; on necessity of divine help, 22; on sin, 115 f.

Plotinus, 39 ff.

Politics in Platonic system, 23

Prayer, in system of Plotinus, 39

Providence, 110 f.

Rationalism, and Greek philosophy, 18 ff.; and Hellenic culture, 8 ff.;

in Epicureanism, 32 f.; meaning of, xi; religion, xi

Religion, and the findings of science, 97; and the scientific age, 97 ff.; Greek, rationalist idea of, 1; Hocking on, 132; Leuba on psychological, 155; meaning of, xiii; meaning of the word, 153 ff.; natural, 153 f.; of Christ, unique character of, 148 f.; of Spinoza, 45 ff.; personal salvation and history, 131 ff.; rationalism a, xi; without God, of Bertrand Russell, 69 ff.

Rite, 158

Rogers, Canon Guy, 143

Ruskin, John, 134

Russell, Bertrand, 157 f.; the god of, viii; religion of, 69 ff.

Salvation, in Spinozan system, 50 f.; personal, religion, history and, 131 ff.; Ruskin's symbol of, 134

Schleiermacher, meaning of religion for, 156

Science, believer's attitude toward, 98 f.; difference between, and philosophy, 99; findings of, and religion, 97 f.

Sin, action of, on will, 118; Greek idea of, 13 ff.; idea of, in Stoicism, 36 f.; in the religion of Wells, 92 ff.; in Spinozan system, 55 f.; in system of Plotinus, 40; moral conscience, and law, 115 ff.; Plato on, 115 f.; Plato's idea of, 24

Socrates, 18 ff.

Sophocles, theology of, 17

Spinoza, 45 ff.; criticism of doctrine of, 48 ff.; ethics in *Short Treatise*, 63 ff.; ethics of, 57 ff.; the god of, viii

Steuart, Rev. H., 98

Stoicism, 33 ff.; idea of sin in, 36 f.; modern, 35

Suffering, hate of, 102 f.

Taylor, A. E., 112 ff., 141; on eternity, 127

Themistocles, on justice, 14

Thomas Aquinas, St., 9

Time, value of, 124 ff.

Tragedy, in Freeman's religion, 74 f.

Unreason, Russell's religion of, 80 ff.

Vanderlaan, 97; quoted, 101

Victorinus, 2 f.

Virtue, in Spinozan system, 47 f.

Wells, H. G., 84 ff.; the god of, viii

Whole, the, in the system of Russell, 73 ff., 82 f.

World, meaning of, for Spinoza, 47; Russell's view of, 74

Worship, Freeman's, of Bertrand Russell, 70, 71 ff.; of infinity, 76 ff.